From Chaos to Continuity

From Chaos to Continuity

THE EVOLUTION OF
LOUISIANA'S JUDICIAL SYSTEM
1712–1862

Mark F. Fernandez

LOUISIANA STATE UNIVERSITY PRESS

Baton Rouge

Published by Louisiana State University Press
Copyright © 2001 by Louisiana State University Press
All rights reserved
Manufactured in the USA
Louisiana Paperback Edition, 2014

DESIGNER: Amanda McDonald Scallan
TYPEFACE: Granjon
TYPEFACE: Coghill Composition Co.

LIBRARY OF CONGRESS CATALOGING-IN-PUBLICATION DATA

Fernandez, Mark F., 1958–
 From chaos to continuity : the evolution of Louisiana's judicial system, 1712–1862 / Mark F. Fernandez.
  p. cm.
Includes bibliographical references and index.
 ISBN 978-0-8071-5685-8 (pbk. : alk. paper) — ISBN 978-0-8071-5686-5 (pdf) —
ISBN 978-0-8071-5687-2 (epub) — ISBN 978-0-8071-5688-9 (mobi)
 1. Justice, Administration of—Louisiana—History. 2. Courts—Louisiana—History.
3. Judges—Louisiana—History.
 KFL78.F47 2001
 347.763—dc21

2001002198

For Dione

Contents

Acknowledgments

This book was born nearly two decades ago in Warren M. Billings's pro-seminar on American legal history at the University of New Orleans. I thank the talented students from that class for the encouragement and ideas that have sustained my efforts ever since. John E. Selby believed in the work as he guided my dissertation at the College of William and Mary. His thoughtful criticism shaped the course of the book. Each member of my dissertation committee—Thad W. Tate, James P. Whittenburg, Charles F. Hobson, and Warren M. Billings—provided valuable criticism at a crucial stage in the book's evolution.

Over the years, countless archivists and librarians have assisted my research. I owe special debts to Carol Billings of the Louisiana Law Library; Wayne Everard of the New Orleans City Archives of the Louisiana Division of the New Orleans Public Library; Margaret Cook from the Special Collections and Manuscript Department at the Earl Gregg Swem Library at the College of William and Mary; E. Lee Shepard from the Virginia Historical Society; the staff at the Library of Virginia and the Alderman Library at the University of Virginia; the Firestone Library at Princeton University; Kevin Hourighan from the Tulane Law Library; and the staff at the Loyola Law Library. They all provided invaluable and timely assistance.

Marie Windell of the Special Collections and Manuscript Division of the Earl K. Long Library at the University of New Orleans deserves special recognition. Marie has lovingly tended the manuscript collection of the Supreme Court of Louisiana since the 1970s. Her oft unnoticed dedication has made the New Louisiana Legal History possible.

My colleagues in the Department of History at Loyola University New

Orleans have made writing this book a joy. Their patience and camaraderie have sustained me over the long process. I owe a special debt of gratitude to my late colleague Peter J. Cangelosi. Deans Robert J. Rowland and Frank E. Scully offered encouragement and support. The Grants and Leaves Committee at Loyola made possible a necessary trip to the Firestone Library. Robbie Meredith, lab assistant extraordinaire, provided useful computer assistance at a crucial time in this book's development. Our department work-study assistant Jarret Winum diligently copied documents for me on request.

Good friends in the field of Louisiana history and the New Legal History have made this task an enjoyable one, especially at the conferences in which these chapters evolved. I thank especially the Billingses (Warren and Carol), Richard H. Kilbourne, Jr. (especially for comments on a very early draft of chapter 2 and for inspiring the approach taken in chapter 4), Jon Kukla, and Judith K. Schafer.

The folks at Louisiana State University Press have been especially supportive. I am particularly indebted to Sylvia Frank for her careful shepherding of the manuscript as well as her enthusiastic encouragement. My copy editors, Gerry Anders and Elizabeth Simon, contributed greatly to the final product.

Warren Billings has been my mentor and adviser through this entire project. I'm even more fortunate to call him a friend.

My family has endured through my anxiety over this book for far too long. Antoinette Fernandez, Vera Hellmers, and Clara Hellmers always seemed aware enough to know when to ask questions and when to keep their curiosity quiet. My wife, Dione, nurtured this book and me through years of fitful starts and stops. My son, Wesley, has distracted me time and again as I prepared this manuscript. I shall treasure those distractions.

INTRODUCTION

Law, Society, and Louisiana's Courts

L aw and society bond in an intricate dance. Law courts provide the stage while litigants, lawyers, judges, and politicians perform, each to their own capabilities, a dazzling array of gestures and poses. Sometimes the performance is graceful and consistent, at other times, clumsy and erratic. The result, no matter how brilliant or amateurish, mirrors the essence of society because the manner in which individuals and corporations resolve their disputes speaks to the very nature of civilization.

Every known human community has either written its own laws or relied on the collective memory of its inhabitants to define the limits and regulations of its society. But laws alone do not illustrate much about a particular culture. Statutes remain on the books long after their particular usefulness has disappeared, customary conventions influence legal commentary merely because they concerned a previous generation of thinkers, and legal principles by themselves are stationary without devices to prime their movements. Courts and jurisprudence, however, provide the instruments needed to interpret the workaday problems and solutions that underscore the rhythms of the dance between law and society.

Scholars have applied numerous devices to elucidate the dance. Investigation of jurisprudence and judicial institutions, however, has not been a source for vigorous study. Although many outstanding studies of the Supreme Court of the United States and federal courts are available, little is known of the origins and development of early state tribunals. Indeed, few students have paid any attention to the development of state government in the early national period.

One promising approach to the study of early state government is to include law and legal culture in the general scheme of state politics. The role of the judiciary garners a major segment of the study of the origin and development of state government. Courts not only represent a central feature of the American political system, but the men and women who sit on those courts and argue before them often use their legal background as a point of entry into the avenues of power. Members of the elite often acquire judicial positions through their political clout and, in turn, use their judicial appointments to maintain their cultural hegemony. Moreover, courts represent the arena where ordinary individuals realize their most important contacts with the state. An examination of the role and development of state courts, accordingly, provides something much more important than a mere history of the law. Historians can observe the subtle contest between competing and complementary elites at their most elementary level through the study of courts and their accompanying culture. Creation of courts within states, subsequent practice and procedure, and the role of the bench in defining a given state's legal culture offer a rich fund of interpretational devices. Examination of those state courts, then, allows for a sweeping analysis of law, society, culture, politics, conflict, and consensus.

At first glance, Louisiana's court system may seem an odd choice for such endeavor. Its diverse Creole culture and civilian heritage have led historians to conclude that Louisiana's legal system is an anachronism in American law. Homegrown historians have reveled in the minutiae of its uniqueness, and mainstream American legal scholars have shied away from studying Louisiana because of its civilian traditions. Even scholars of codification in America have shunned the study of Louisiana, arguing that its civilian legal system differs too much from the marriage of codes and common law that typified American practice in the nineteenth century. These scholars have misinterpreted the origins of Louisiana's legal system.[1]

---

1. Lawrence M. Friedman stated that Louisiana has no common law heritage, in *American Law: An Introduction* (New York: W. W. Norton, 1984), 44. In *The American Codification*

When the French prefect Pierre Clément de Laussat arrived in Louisiana to receive the colony from Spain, he suspended all the offices of the Spanish government. Since he did not have time to restructure the legal system before turning Louisiana over to the Americans, the United States acquired a territory devoid of laws and legal institutions. Nonetheless, the territory's *ancienne population* retained its allegiance to civilian legal customs. Louisiana's entry into the United States required the extension of certain constitutional guarantees, some of them firmly rooted in the Anglo-American tradition of justice. President Thomas Jefferson and the men he chose as territorial officials wanted to impose a representative American system of law and justice on the new territory to speed up its Americanization. Jefferson, however, was a practical man. Believing that wholesale destruction of the civilian system might spark resistance to the American administration, Jefferson advised his officials to pursue a cautious policy that ensured basic American liberties and encouraged the reception of American judicial principles, yet allowed the *ancienne population* to retain many of its familiar legal traditions.

On the whole, Jefferson's policy succeeded largely through the efforts of a bench and bar dominated by Americans, especially on the high appellate level. The study of Louisiana's law courts and its legal culture in the early national period chronicles the success of Jefferson's policy. In comparison to other southern states of the period, this investigation of Louisiana shows it to be a representative model of an Anglo-American common law jurisdiction sharing remarkably similar experiences with its neighboring jurisdictions.

Because Louisiana's judicial history has not attracted the attention of many scholars, the chronicle of the state's courts largely has been left unwritten. The few studies of Louisiana's courts that have appeared usually

---

Movement: A Study of Antebellum Legal Reform (Westport, Conn.: Greenwood Press, 1981), Charles M. Cook argued that Louisiana's codification movement was ancillary to the movement in America's common law, stating: "it occurred in its own very special milieu quite independent of law reforms elsewhere," x. For a full-blown discussion/critique of Louisiana's legal historiography see Mark F. Fernandez, "Louisiana's Legal History: Its Past, Present, and Future," in Warren M. Billings and Mark F. Fernandez, *A Law unto Itself? Essays in the New Louisiana Legal History* (Baton Rouge: Louisiana State University Press, 2001).

have been of a general nature. Louisiana's early courts have been all but neglected.

Louisiana's high court of appeals presents an even more challenging topic. Most of Louisiana's legal history consists of specialized studies of the fine points of civil law in legal publications. Since this literature is so prevalent and so specialized, it has caused historians to interpret Louisiana as a unique, almost mystical jurisdiction whose study is open only to civil law experts. Moreover, this emphasis on the subtleties of the civilian jurisdiction has obscured contributions of the common law to Louisiana's legal heritage. Much of the history of that common law reveals itself through the study of the state's appellate courts.[2]

Thus, the study of Louisiana's judicial system in the early national and antebellum periods offers important clues not only to the origins of state government, but also to judicial development. To execute such a study, however, two important questions must be considered.

What can the study of such a seemingly disparate jurisdiction do to forward an understanding of the legal history of the American South? To answer that question, it is necessary to look at the similarities between Louisiana and other southern jurisdictions. Most of the antebellum southern states, including Louisiana, grew out of colonial settlements that, for different reasons, occurred rather abruptly, leaving the door open for revolutionary legal evolution. In all cases, and in varying degrees, the states adopted judicial organs that allowed for sweeping changes in their legal systems. All states also retained important traditional aspects of their colonial legal orders. The resulting legal cultures, accordingly, reflected both revolutionary and conservative elements of legal evolution.

In stable societies, law—both of civilian and common law origins—represents a traditional and conservative force. Change occurs slowly and is usually initiated by a legal and constitutional order that is dominated by a conservative, lawyer-dominated segment of society. But revolutions in law are frequent, if not prevalent, events in history. Scholars of com-

2. Warren M. Billings, "Louisiana Legal History and Its Sources: Needs, Opportunities, and Approaches," in Edward F. Haas, ed., *Louisiana's Legal Heritage* (New Orleans: Perdido Bay Press, 1983), 189–202.

parative law posit four sets of occasions that encourage such innovative change—when tradition has made the law "cumbrous and remote from social realities"; when there is a "realistic possibility" of borrowing from foreign systems; in cases of political and social revolution; and when a forceful ruling elite uses law as its instrument for a radical reshaping of society.[3]

The creation of judicial institutions in the South produced both traditional and revolutionary changes in the realm of law and legal institutions. Traditional influences, namely the common law in the other southern states and Louisiana's civilian heritage, remained strong throughout the revolutionary phases of these early states' legal and constitutional history. Not only were they prevalent among members of the legal community, but they also remained strong among the multifarious groups that made up the states' social, political, and economic fabric.

Louisiana's legal history following the Louisiana Purchase reveals a similar experience. Traditional forces encouraged the retention of many civilian aspects of private law, but cumbrous practices, especially in the judicial realm, offered openings for common law intrusions. Attention to changing social realities also affected the reception of certain common law devices. American constitutional guarantees of trial by jury and habeas corpus, for instance, necessitated the adaptation of legal principles revolutionary to Louisiana. Borrowing from American and English legal structures became not only possible but also practical as lawyers and judges trained in American law gained control of Louisiana's bar. When Jefferson purchased the colony and Congress provided for American forms of government and representation, and as immigrants poured into the region from American dominions, a political and social revolution occurred. Finally, both territorial officials and leading members of Louisiana's legal elite desired to use the law as a tool to shape the state into a representative model of American justice. That they sought to do so cautiously and in moderate terms reflects Jefferson's eagerness to provide a smooth assimilation of Louisiana into the United States. The caution and conciliation of

3. These conditions are discussed thoroughly in Alan Watson, *The Evolution of Law* (Baltimore: Johns Hopkins University Press, 1985), see esp. 110–4.

the president, his successor, and their territorial appointees should not obscure the fact that they eventually hoped to turn Louisiana into a model of American justice.

Thus, the study of Louisiana's judicial history offers much in the way of studying legal stability and change in the early republic. Moreover, the resulting legal orders in the southern states bear many striking procedural and substantive similarities. For Louisiana such similarities suggest a revision of contemporary notions of the state's role in the American legal system.

What can such study reveal about colonial and antebellum Louisiana? This analysis will argue that Louisiana's legal order should not be viewed as an anomaly in the American judicial system.

Questions of legal history notwithstanding, the examination will shed light on important and overlooked aspects of the political, intellectual, economic, and social character of the Louisiana community. Since courts represent the most active arena in which citizens and the state interact, the history of judicial bodies—especially in regard to constitutional, ideological, and mundane forms of litigation—illustrates not only the challenges faced by growing communities, but also the intellectual and pragmatic ways in which they resolve them.

Courts are political creations: Judges are either elected or owe their appointments to elected officials; lawyers depend on the leadership of judges to regulate their professional associations, to police their ethical standards, and to establish and enforce procedure; and the legal establishment itself often produces the politicians who direct the legal system from state and national capitals. Consequently, a consideration of the background, education, and ideological allegiance of the state's judges in the antebellum period forms a major part of the investigation.

As John C. Calhoun pointed out in the nineteenth century, law serves a universal purpose in society—to protect the individual from the community and vice versa.[4] Communities need not adopt a specific legal sys-

---

4. John C. Calhoun, "Disquisition on Government," in *Works of John C. Calhoun*, vol. 1 (New York: n.p., 1863), 15, 16, 25; this is analyzed carefully in James Willard Hurst, *The Growth of American Law: The Lawmakers* (Boston: Little, Brown, 1950), 439–47.

tem; rather, they should employ an accepted form of regulation to direct individual and corporate relationships. Application of civilian or common law principles is actually unimportant to the development of social stability. Nonetheless, the choice of one system over another speaks directly to the character of a particular society—whether it allows its legal community to interpret and to innovate on its law via the courts through the consistent use of precedent, or whether it binds its lawyers and judges through an inflexible series of codes.

In the South nearly two centuries of settlement had established the ascendancy of common law. But in the late eighteenth century, the civil law gained respectability and attractiveness. By the early nineteenth century, calls for uniform codes began to echo in the region's halls of justice. Louisiana's judicial history, in contrast, began with civilian precepts, and only in the nineteenth century did American and English precedents begin to inform its judicial discourse. Still, the attraction of the civil law remained prominent, especially among Louisiana's Creoles and their political allies. The initial stages of this comparison, accordingly, reveal a system moving ever closer to the conception of a mixed jurisdiction. That Louisiana arrived at that juncture earlier in its history than other states merely reflects the break with tradition orchestrated by the Purchase.

Such profound legal changes have less to do with communal attitudes and ideologies than with the role of lawmakers in their respective societies. The judges, lawyers, and politicians of any particular community determine the extent to which the law is written, applied, and interpreted. Thus, in the legal realm of society, change moves usually from the "top down." Society's elite read the law and their ideological and environmental worldviews inform their readings.[5]

Students of Louisiana's judicial organization must attend to the battle

---

5. A strong case for this interpretation of change in the law is in Arthur A. Leff, "Injury, Ignorance, and Spite—The Dynamics of Coercive Collection," *Yale Law Journal* (November 1970): 1–46. Nonetheless, it is evident that social conditions may also force changes in the law from the "bottom up" as the courts respond to various upheavals in society. Excellent examples of this phenomenon may be seen in Eugene D. Genovese, *Roll Jordan Roll* (New York: Pantheon Books, 1975) and E. P. Thompson, *Whigs and Hunters: The Origin of the Black Act* (New York: Pantheon Books, 1975).

for cultural hegemony reflected in the ideologies of the members of the bench and bar. The study of these elites in competition along the lines of such a battle will allow for the incorporation of both ideological and environmental considerations.[6] Thus, the nineteenth-century movement from "moral" or republican legal principles to more practical applications may be glimpsed in its social context via the examination of the institutional development of Louisiana's judicial bodies.[7]

Any story reads best when begun at the beginning. This book starts with a brief overview of the long and diverse colonial legacy of Louisiana's judicial system. The question of how Anglo-American principles became part of Louisiana's legal heritage, though, provides the central focus for the investigation, so the majority of this work centers on the period following the Louisiana Purchase. The impact of Anglo-American legal principles on Louisiana and of civilian precepts on American jurisdictions started during the early national period. Louisiana emerged as the first jurisdiction to confront American jurists with the problem of integrating the two systems of law, but the confrontation continued throughout the United States in the nineteenth century. Investigation of Louisiana's legal system, then, provides a useful frame of reference for scholars interested in the development of law and justice in the American South and West.

6. The flexibility of the cultural hegemony theory is hailed in T. J. Jackson Lears, "The Concept of Cultural Hegemony: Problems and Possibilities," *American Historical Review* (June 1985): 567–94; and the effectiveness of using the model for a top-down approach is considered in John Patrick Diggins, "The Misuses of Gramsci," *Journal of American History* (June 1988): 141–5.

7. An excellent example of this type of analysis in Kentucky's federal district courts is Sandra F. VanBurkleo, "'That Our Pure Republican Principles Might Not Whither': Kentucky's Relief Crisis and the Pursuit of 'Moral Justice,' 1818–1826" (Ph.D. diss., University of Minnesota, 1988).

From Chaos to Continuity

I

FRENCHMEN AND SPANIARDS
The Colonial Period

On 26 September 1712, Louisiana became a civilian jurisdiction when Louis XIV granted Antoine Crozat letters patent to "all the territory possessed by the Crown between old and new Mexico and Carolina." Before that time the colony was subject to military rule. Crozat's grant marked a turning point in the colony's development by ushering in a period of conciliar rule that established Louisiana's first judicial system. Separate edicts of 12 and 23 December 1712 set up a temporary Superior Council that on 16 September 1716 gave way to a more permanent eight-man council.[1]

The edict that created the Superior Council granted it jurisdiction in all civil and criminal causes. The *commissaire-ordonnateur*[2] served as the

1. Ben Robertson Miller, *The Louisiana Judiciary* (Baton Rouge: Louisiana State University Press, 1932), 1; François-Xavier Martin, *The History of Louisiana from the Earliest Period,* vol. 1 (New Orleans: Lyman and Beardslee, 1827–1829), 178. Two excellent surveys of the Superior Council are James D. Hardy, Jr., "The Superior Council in Colonial Louisiana," in John Francis McDermott, ed., *Frenchmen and French Ways in the Mississippi Valley* (Urbana: University of Illinois Press, 1969), 87–103; and Jerry A. Micelle's "From Law Court to Local Government: Metamorphosis of the Superior Council of French Louisiana," *Louisiana History* 9 (spring 1968): 85–107. A solid brief description of the council may be found in Henry Plauché Dart, "The Legal Institutions of Louisiana," *Louisiana Historical Quarterly* 2 (January 1919): 72–103.

2. Donald Jile Lemieux, "The Office of *Commissaire Ordonnateur* in French Louisiana, 1731–1763: A Study in French Colonial Administration" (Ph.D. diss., Louisiana State University, 1972), vii.

honorary president of the council, but in practice a senior councilor presided over the court. He alone sat as the court of first instance in provisional actions, while a quorum of three was necessary. A five-man quorum determined criminal matters. Meeting monthly, the council operated in exactly the same fashion as those in other French colonies, such as St. Domingue and Martinique.[3]

When in 1717 the Western Company, a joint-stock venture, assumed Crozat's charter, it added a system of inferior courts to assist the council in its judicial duties. If the Western Company found itself involved in a civil suit, then the case was heard in the Consular Jurisdiction of Paris with appeals before the Parlement of Paris.[4]

In September 1719 the crown revised the Western Company's charter to accommodate the rapid growth experienced by the colony after Bienville's founding of New Orleans. Under the amended charter the council heard appeals from the inferior courts with the king reserving the right to review conciliar decrees. After 1719 the Superior Council began to exercise administrative authority in a variety of capacities, and its officers joined forces with military interests in the colony. Eventually, the council asserted legislative prerogatives far beyond the ambit of its powers as described in the initial edicts.[5] In 1731 Louis XV attempted to prohibit such lawmaking discretion, but the Superior Council, separated from direct royal interference by distance and lack of interest, continued to wield such authority as late as 1743.[6] The council's exercise of legislative and administrative powers often invited controversy, but its judicial authority remained unchallenged throughout the Western Company's checkered existence.[7] Thus, the development of the colony's courts had an uncharacteristic record of success.

3. Miller, *Louisiana Judiciary*, 2; Martin, *History of Louisiana*, 180–2.

4. Miller, *Louisiana Judiciary*, 2; Martin, *History of Louisiana*, 198.

5. Micelle, "From Law Court to Local Government," 85–107.

6. See "Ordinance of the Superior Council Regulating the Practice of Medicine, Surgery, and Obstetrics," in "The Cabildo Archives," *Louisiana Historical Quarterly* 3 (January–October, 1920): 86.

7. A good discussion of the internecine struggles to administer the colony is contained in Charles Edwards O'Neill's *Church and State in French Colonial Louisiana: Policy and Politics to 1732* (New Haven: Yale University Press, 1966).

By the late 1720s the French had organized the inferior courts into nine efficient judicial districts: Alibamons, Mobile, Biloxi, New Orleans, Natchez, the Yazoos, the Illinois and Wabash, Arkansas, and Natchitoches. Inferior courts within these districts consisted of a director or agent of the company assisted by two local magistrates.[8]

In 1729, Indian warfare led the Western Company to abandon its hopes of making Louisiana profitable, and in July 1731 it relinquished its title to the monarch. In May 1732 the crown reorganized its possession, creating a thirteen-man Superior Council with members of that body serving as "assessors" in cases of first instance.[9] Relying on a loose interpretation of the *Coutumes de Paris* and royal edicts, this form of judicial organization remained in effect until the revolt of 1768.[10]

France stumbled through a series of imperial wars and continental entanglements throughout the eighteenth century. As a result, Louis XV's ministers occupied themselves with warfare, and Louisiana experienced a period of "salutary neglect" similar to that of the British North American colonies in the age of Walpole.[11] Viewing Louisiana as a poor stepchild to the richer reserves of New France, Louis XV allowed the officials and citizens of Louisiana to fend for themselves in a variety of political and administrative venues. That the council often served as a vehicle for such

8. Miller, *Louisiana Judiciary*, 2–3; Martin, *History of Louisiana*, 198, 245; Dart, "Legal Institutions of Louisiana," 91.

9. Miller, *Louisiana Judiciary*, 3; Martin, *History of Louisiana*, 215–6.

10. Although the council remained active until Antonio de Ulloa contrived to abolish it after Spain took control of the colony. For a brief analysis of the evolution of the *Coutumes de Paris* and its application in Louisiana, see Jerah Johnson, "*Les Coutumes de Paris*, Louisiana's First Law," *Louisiana History* 30 (spring 1989): 145–55.

11. Historians of colonial British North America often characterize Walpole's administration as a time of "salutary neglect," building on Edmund Burke's classic statement. Some historians of early America, such as James Henretta, have challenged that interpretation. Nonetheless, the general term, meaning that the mother country had ignored the colonial region to the extent that its inhabitants were able to conduct their own affairs without much interference, seems to work for mid-eighteenth-century Louisiana quite well. See W. A. Speck, "The International and Imperial Context," in *Colonial British America: Essays in the New History of the Early Modern Era*, ed. Jack P. Greene and J. R. Pole (Baltimore: Johns Hopkins University Press, 1984), 398–401.

maneuvering should not be surprising. In British and in Dutch North America, the distance between the metropolitan center and the colonial peripheries often facilitated a blending of governmental prerogatives in both legislative and judicial institutions.[12] Despite the disputed nature of the Superior Council's administrative history, it provided for a high degree of excellence, often exceeding the quality of the mother country's courts in both civil and criminal causes.[13]

After the Seven Years' War, France ceded the colony to Spain to compensate the Spanish Bourbons for their support. When Louisiana became a Spanish colony in 1762, logistical problems and the messy nature of Spain's own imperial bureaucracy prevented Spain from taking immediate possession of its new acquisition. Accordingly, Spain allowed the administration of Louisiana to fend for itself from 1762 to 1766, when Antonio de Ulloa finally assumed control of Louisiana for Charles III.[14]

Of all the candidates Charles III could have chosen to govern Louisiana, Antonio de Ulloa was the worst. A slender, bookish man, young Ulloa gravitated toward intellectual pursuits. He was an excellent student, reveling in his studies, especially in mathematics and the natural sciences, but his scholarly endeavors provided little training for more vigorous activities, such as military service. Unfortunately, only limited opportunities existed for lesser nobles like Ulloa in eighteenth-century Spain. Many chose the military as a path to career advancement. Lacking the stature and stamina for combat, Ulloa relied on his intelligence and innate meticulousness to cut his path through the Spanish naval academy. His educational success presented Ulloa with his first career opportunity as a soldier. In 1734 he signed on as a military escort and mathematician to a Parisian

12. For British North America, the best discussion of this aspect of constitutional development is in Jack P. Greene, *Peripheries and Center: Constitutional Development in the Extended Politics of the British Empire and the United States, 1607–1788* (Athens: University of Georgia Press, 1986). For the Dutch experience, see Michael Kammen, *Colonial New York: A History* (White Plains, N.Y.: KTO Press, 1975).

13. John Preston Moore, *Revolt in Louisiana: The Spanish Occupation, 1766–1770* (Baton Rouge: Louisiana State University Press, 1976), 32, 29n; cf. James D. Hardy, Jr., "Superior Council in Colonial Louisiana," 101.

14. Moore, *Revolt in Louisiana,* 34–40.

expedition to Ecuador in search of the equator. The success of the quest opened doors for other exploratory ventures. Soon Ulloa won renown for naturalist studies of the Americas coauthored with his brother, Juan. In typical Enlightenment fashion, Ulloa's superiors, impressed with his scientific accomplishments, appointed him to an administrative position. So, in 1758, Ulloa traveled to Peru to reform Huancavelica, a foundering mining province. Although Ulloa's plans to revitalize the mining industry were sensible, his brusque leadership style and overbearing attention to economy and detail roused opposition in the graft-ridden region. In 1764, his opponents engineered his ouster.[15]

On 5 March 1766, a defeated but dogmatic Ulloa arrived on a rain-swept New Orleans levee. Hoping to redeem himself for the Huancavelica debacle, Ulloa strove to assimilate Louisiana into the Spanish empire. Unfortunately, his meticulous, scientific nature fueled procrastination and indecision. Ulloa's failure to embrace the local elite and his inability to compromise also helped to stymie his efforts to control the colony.[16] Such control was essential given the reservations that most Louisianians shared about the cession of the colony to Spain.

Neglected by the French since 1762, the commercial establishment in Louisiana had repeatedly petitioned Louis XV to undo the transfer of the colony, most notably by sending Jean Milhet, a prominent merchant, to the French court.[17] Mainly the merchants feared that the Spaniards would institute legal reforms that could dispossess them of their holdings and place them firmly "under the yoke of Spain."[18] Ulloa's drive to reorganize the legal system exacerbated those fears. He committed his first mistake immediately on his arrival by failing to take formal possession of the colony. Accordingly, Ulloa's regime in the ensuing months assumed the air of a provisional government, one that was preparing the way for major

15. Ibid., 2–8.

16. Ibid., 34–40; John Preston Moore, "Antonio de Ulloa: A Profile of the First Spanish Governor of Louisiana," *Louisiana History* 8 (summer 1967): 200–1; Carl A. Brasseaux, *Denis-Nicolas Foucault and the New Orleans Rebellion of 1768* (Ruston, La.: McGinty: 1987), 50–2.

17. Moore, *Revolt in Louisiana,* 40.

18. Martin, *History of Louisiana,* 353.

changes on the occasion of official retrocession. The prospect of such reforms frightened Louisiana's French citizens and made them dread the formal assumption of Spanish leadership.[19]

In January 1767, after shoring up the Spanish military presence, Ulloa further alarmed the French citizenry when he moved to dissolve the Superior Council, which had fallen into the hands of a corrupt junto after 1762. The shunned council, consisting of the most influential leaders of the opposition, believed that their worst fears were materializing. To abolish the council, Ulloa persuaded his superior, Jeronimo Grimaldi, to draft a royal decree to reorganize the colony's legal system. Believing that Louisiana had no reason to expect an independent judiciary since other Spanish possessions, such as Havana, did not have them, Ulloa urged Grimaldi to vest judicial power in the governor alone. Then, according to Spanish imperial practices, the governor would preside over all civil and criminal appeals with the assistance of a trained lawyer called an *asesor letrado.* On retrocession, then, the Superior Council would cease to exist, and the governor would become the supreme judicial official.[20]

Ulloa also urged Grimaldi to draft far-reaching reforms of the colony's administration. A revised municipal code covering religion, manners, provisions, public health, and public safety formed the core of the administrative changes. Although Grimaldi modeled the *titres,* or sections of the code, after similar provisions for the West Indies, the French inhabitants of New Orleans interpreted the comprehensive nature of the document, along with the proposed dissolution of the council, as a clear threat to their autonomy. Moreover, in the public safety section, the prudent retention of French troops in outlying Indian territories, under their popular commander, Governor Charles Philippe Aubry, raised the hackles of both Indian and British leaders on the frontier.[21]

Since the end of the Seven Years' War, the British had been stepping up their military activities in West Florida. Strategic location of English forces along Louisiana's eastern border greatly concerned Ulloa. His first

19. Ibid., 352; Brasseaux, *Foucault,* 52.
20. Moore, *Revolt in Louisiana,* 42–59.
21. Ibid., 40–53; Martin, *History of Louisiana,* 355.

response was to strengthen the forts along the Mississippi. Although Ulloa achieved a measure of success, still he worried that the forts alone would not repel a concerted invasion. To provide extra security for the port, he limited traffic on the river to a single channel. Ulloa's efforts, with the help of diplomatic cooperation from Great Britain, largely succeeded in ending hostilities between the two empires. Restricting river traffic, however, precipitated a wave of opposition from New Orleans merchants. The northeastern channel that Ulloa kept open had a reputation of being one of the territory's most difficult waters to navigate. Furthermore, reduction of the number of open channels considerably slowed the port's commercial activities, hitting Ulloa's critics in that most delicate part of their anatomy—the purse.[22]

With the English at bay, Ulloa turned his attention to the Indians. When the Spanish assumed control of Louisiana, they realized that capitalizing on the colony's lively Indian trade was crucial to the success of the venture. Wary that radical change might lead to violence, Ulloa, with Aubry's support, maintained the French policy of friendship with the Indians. Mimicking effective British techniques, Ulloa sought to stifle the traders' abuse of the Indians through strict commercial regulation. He set high penalties for violation of Spanish ordinances and enlisted the French commandant at St. Louis, Louis St. Ange, to enforce them. By 1768 rigid enforcement of Ulloa's regulatory policies had begun to alienate the region's French traders, adding their voices to the already stout opposition front.[23]

Spain had acquired Louisiana in hopes of turning it into a profitable enterprise, so it was not surprising that Ulloa's early reforms included commercial regulations. Any shift of a colony's imperial center would call for a redefinition of its trading policies. In 1766, Ulloa, via Aubry, submitted a decree to the Superior Council that would require shipmasters to obtain licenses and passports from the Spanish government in order to en-

22. Moore, *Revolt in Louisiana*, 68–73.

23. Ibid., 103–23; Daniel Usner, *Indians, Settlers, and Slaves in a Frontier Exchange Economy: The Lower Mississippi Valley before 1783* (Chapel Hill: University of North Carolina Press, 1992), 118.

gage in trade. Although this paralleled routine antismuggling measures in the Spanish empire, such comprehensive regulation shocked and enraged the French commercial community, which had built much of its fortune on illicit trade with Great Britain.[24]

The proposed changes in the judicial system, coupled with the military and regulatory provisions of the revised municipal code, caused great dissatisfaction among Louisiana's already suspicious French citizenry. That the new provisions attacked the livelihood of Louisiana's most prosperous and influential citizens made the situation volatile. In creating those provisions, Ulloa alienated the very segment of the population whose support he needed most to effect a smooth transition. By the winter of 1768, relations between Ulloa and his constituents had deteriorated to such an extent that the Louisianians began scheming to rid themselves of the troublesome governor. When a monetary crisis left the colony in desperate financial straits, the schemers set their plots in motion.[25]

From the beginning of the Spanish occupation, the crown had endeavored to retire French currency from the economy and to replace it with Spanish money. Unfortunately, a dearth of Spanish specie and Ulloa's refusal to underwrite a debt of 2,683,000 livres led to a depreciation of French currency and a wave of inflation. To combat the inflation, Ulloa issued Spanish notes, but this measure met with only partial success. Anticipating the importation of large quantities of Spanish specie to relieve the crisis, Ulloa sought to diminish the role of France's commissary, Denis-Nicolas Foucault, reducing him to the status of a mere "executor and caretaker of governmental property," and limiting his duties to "settling the accounts of the French administration and assembling an inventory of the properties to be taken over by the Spanish, for which indemnification was to be made."[26] Although Foucault's demotion freed him to focus on the muddled state of the colony's finances, Ulloa had essentially emasculated the one French official who could and would come to his aid in a crisis.[27]

24. Brasseaux, *Foucault,* 69–73; Moore, *Revolt in Louisiana,* 103–42.
25. Brasseaux, *Foucault,* 69–73; Moore, *Revolt in Louisiana,* 103–42.
26. Moore, *Revolt in Louisiana,* 127.
27. Brasseaux, *Foucault,* 71–2.

Appropriations from Spain, however, came slowly and in cut-rate increments. In October 1768, Ulloa found himself with only half of the pesos necessary to meet his payroll and operating expenses. By the end of the month, Louisiana was in a dire financial position. Shortage of specie had combined with the decline in trade resulting from Ulloa's commercial policies to threaten the stability of the Spanish government.[28] To complicate matters, Louisiana had recently witnessed the influx of a variety of new immigrants, each grasping for a share of the already shrinking pie. During this wave of immigration many English and Americans migrated to the region. North Carolinians fleeing the regulator troubles had settled north of New Orleans and established trading and farming communities. English and American entrepreneurs had begun to settle in New Orleans and quickly launched an aggressive campaign that, by the 1790s, would make them the undisputed leaders of the commercial community (needless to say, this development ruffled the feathers of the French merchants). A large farming community of Germans had settled on what came to be known as the German Coast in the mid–eighteenth century. Finally, in 1768 the large-scale relocation of Acadians, fleeing persecution in Nova Scotia, placed further stress on the economy as the Spanish commissary took over from Foucault the burden of maintaining these citizens.[29] As the crisis deepened, the fear of strict enforcement of the new commercial regulations heightened anxiety among the French citizenry. Before the end of October a small but influential group of Louisiana's citizens revolted against Ulloa's authority.

The seeds of the 1768 revolt had taken root in the winter of 1767–68.

---

28. Moore, *Revolt in Louisiana*, 130.

29. Ibid., 134–5; Richard E. Chandler, trans. and ed., "End of an Odyssey: Acadians Arrive at St. Gabriel, Louisiana," *Louisiana History* 14 (winter 1973): 69–87; Light T. Cummins, "Anglo Merchants in Spanish New Orleans: Capital Migration and the Atlantic Economy, 1760–1803" (paper presented at the 53rd meeting of the Southern Historical Association, New Orleans, 13 November 1987); Carl A. Brasseaux, *The Founding of New Acadia: The Beginnings of Acadian Life in Louisiana, 1765–1803* (Baton Rouge: Louisiana State University Press, 1987); Lewis William Newton, *The Americanization of French Louisiana: A Study in American Populations of Louisiana, 1803–1860* (New York: Arno Press, 1980), 1; Martin, *History of Louisiana*, 356–9.

Jean Milhet returned from France bearing the sad news that the colonists could not expect the crown to violate its agreement with Spain. Prospects of a poor spring harvest also led to a wave of dissent in the German Coast. The farmers held meetings regarding Ulloa that winter. They pursued many ideas, the most promising of which involved circulating a petition for the governor's removal, but they took no action. As the financial crisis deepened during the summer, Foucault and the French attorney general, Nicolas Chauvin de La Frenière, met in the garden of Madame Marie Louise de Pradel to discuss ways to thwart the Spanish takeover. At first they sought to enlist the aid of British brigadier general Sir Frederick Haldimand in Pensacola in an effort to liberate the colony. Lacking sufficient might and not wishing to precipitate a clash with Spain, Haldimand rejected their overtures. Undaunted, the ringleaders looked for allies among the citizens.[30]

In the early fall the revolt began in earnest. La Frenière and his confederates drafted a memorial against Ulloa and began collecting signatures. Once a suitable number of citizens signed the memorial, La Frenière and Foucault presented it to the Superior Council. On 28 October Foucault persuaded the council to consider the petition. The following day the council passed the indictment of the Spanish regime and the rebellion began.[31]

Of prime importance to the council's resolution were protests against Ulloa's suggested legal and administrative changes. To validate their actions, the councilors argued that since Ulloa had not dissolved the Superior Council, it could receive the complaints of the people against the governor. Furthermore, the councilors reported that they had found sufficient validity in the grievances of the population to expel the governor. Aubry objected to the council's resolutions, but the councilors ignored his protest.[32]

At 2:00 in the afternoon, just as victory celebrations began in the city, the council's scribe delivered the expulsion order to Ulloa aboard his frig-

30. Moore, *Revolt in Louisiana,* 146–7.
31. Ibid., 154–61.
32. Ibid.

ate, the *Volante*. Ulloa departed for Havana two days later. Although the rebels had succeeded in expelling the hated governor, their resolution declared neither independence nor secession from the Spanish empire. Spanish officials remained in office while the Superior Council assumed loose direction of the day-to-day affairs of the colony.[33] The simple act of rebellion, however, ensured a response from Charles III.

Rather than seek conciliation, Charles III chose to repress the rebellion with brutal, decisive force. He called on the services of a trusted soldier of fortune, Alejandro O'Reilly, who had proved his worth in the Spanish invasion of Portugal during the Seven Years' War. A marked contrast to Ulloa, the Irishman's commanding physical presence and acquired courtly demeanor suited him well for both combat and leadership.[34]

On 24 July 1769, O'Reilly arrived in New Orleans aboard, ironically, the *Volante*. His initial interviews with the councilors led them to believe that Spain had adopted a conciliatory posture. Why should it not? Ulloa's expulsion was little more than a bloodless coup. No violence had taken place against Spain or Spanish officials in New Orleans during the episode. In fact, the councilors had made strong overtures to Ulloa's underlings and had kept them involved in the colony's government after his departure.

O'Reilly took a different view of the situation. In August, bolstered by the arrival of warships, he took formal possession of the colony. He then sweet-talked Aubry into supplying him with the names of the leading conspirators against Ulloa. After identifying the ringleaders, O'Reilly arrested all of them except Foucault. Felix Del Rey, a prosecutor whom O'Reilly had enlisted in Havana while en route to New Orleans, opened proceedings against the insurgents. After charging the defendants and interrogating witnesses, Del Rey individually examined each conspirator.[35]

Meanwhile, O'Reilly had imprisoned Foucault and had tried, fruitlessly, to coax him into confessing his role in the rebellion. As a French official, Foucault, unlike La Frenière and other leaders of the insurrec-

---

33. Ibid., 161–5.
34. Ibid., 190–217; Martin, *History of Louisiana*, 356–9.
35. Moore, *Revolt in Louisiana*, 190–217; Martin, *History of Louisiana*, 356–9.

tion, enjoyed a measure of diplomatic protection. O'Reilly deported him to France and left his fate in the hands of the king.[36] In the end, Del Rey found the conspirators guilty. Six—La Frenière, Jean Baptiste Noyan, Pierre Marquis, Pierre Caresse, Joseph Villeré (who died before the trial was concluded), and Joseph Milhet—received the death penalty. Balthasar Masan, Jerome Doucet, Jean Milhet, Pierre Poupet, and Pierre Hardi de Boisblanc were found guilty of collaborating with the conspirators. Del Rey sentenced Masan and Doucet to six-year prison terms; the rest received ten-year sentences.[37]

On 25 October, soldiers marched the five condemned prisoners into the yard of the Lisbon regiment and carried out the sentence. When the sound of the deadly volley echoed through the halls of the Ursuline convent next door, it signaled the end of France's domination of Louisiana. O'Reilly had engineered the swift and violent demise of the rebellion.[38] Nonetheless, he realized that continued oppression would likely lead to further insurrection. In the months following the executions, he moved swiftly to solidify Spanish rule and supply stable leadership. By removing all remaining French officials, establishing Spanish as the official language, providing for a new legal code, new judicial and administrative systems, and the revitalization of the Catholic church, O'Reilly firmly secured Spain's administrative control of the colony and furnished the residents with the social, economic, political, and religious stability necessary to maintain the peace.

Although his solution to the insurrection earned him the nickname "Bloody O'Reilly," the governor's decisive policies quelled the rebellion and established Spain's undisputed control of the colony. From a legal and judicial standpoint, O'Reilly's administrative reforms composed the core of the system that provided Louisiana with stable conflict resolution until Pierre Clément de Laussat reclaimed the colony for France in 1803.[39]

36. Brasseaux, *Foucault,* 90; David Ker Texada, *Alejandro O'Reilly and the New Orleans Rebels* (Lafayette: University of Southwestern Louisiana, 1970).

37. Moore, *Revolt in Louisiana,* 203–8.

38. Ibid., 208–9.

39. All scholarship on legal reforms in Spanish Louisiana has recently been superseded by the excellent work of Gilbert C. Din and John E. Harkins, *The New Orleans Cabildo: Colonial Louisiana's First City Government, 1769–1803* (Baton Rouge: Louisiana State University Press, 1996).

One of O'Reilly's primary tasks was to create laws in force for the colony that reflected Spanish concerns. To do this, he devised a new system intended to install the laws of the Indies and Castile, mingled with whatever French customs he deemed prudent. Drawing inspiration from the *Recopilación de las Indias,* the *Siete Partidas,* and the French *Code Noir* of 1724, O'Reilly worked out a system that ultimately would serve Louisiana well. To make these new laws accessible to the French inhabitants of Louisiana, in 1769 O'Reilly engaged two lawyers, Del Rey and Manuel José de Urrutia, to redact them into the "Code O'Reilly."[40]

In addition to revising the laws, O'Reilly instituted a host of other legal reforms. He dissolved the Superior Council and established the cabildo as the residence of the administrative and judicial offices of the Spanish government. O'Reilly designed the cabildo to function as an apparatus of mixed government similar to the Superior Council and many bodies in the neighboring British North American colonies. Accordingly, most cabildo offices possessed some judicial authority. In ordering the cabildo, O'Reilly provided for a more thorough administration for Louisiana. O'Reilly's new judicial system, however, radically altered Louisiana's courts.[41]

Unlike the French council, cabildo "judges"[42] heard cases individually. The governor and nearly every cabildo official held some measure of judicial authority. Litigants were divided into two classes: *fueros* (those with special privileges) and *ordinarios* (those without). Spanish courts in the colony recognized these divisions and divided judicial power accordingly. The most important courts heard cases involving *fueros,* a group that included the military, civil officers, and the clergy. At the top end of this system the governor served on a plethora of tribunals. He sat on the military court that heard courts-martial and cases involving military personnel and civilians. From 1769 to 1780 the Governor's Court also heard treasury cases. In 1780 the crown created an Intendant's Court to hear treasury

40. Ibid., 101–2.
41. Ibid., 102.
42. The term *judges* here must be used with the understanding that these cabildo officials possessed other administrative functions as well. They should be viewed in this context as royal officials wearing "judicial hats."

matters. Between 1788 and 1794, however, Governors Miró and Carondelet served as "governors-intendant" and thus sat on the Intendant's Court as well. The other *fuero* court was the Ecclesiastical Court, established in 1772, which dealt with matters regarding marriage and cases involving religion, church retainers, and the church's slaves.[43]

Complementing the *fuero* courts were those of the *alcaldes ordinarios*.[44] These tribunals served both as courts of first instance and as appeals for individuals who did not possess a *fuero*. The *alcaldes ordinarios* also had criminal jurisdiction over a range of offenses from petty to capital cases, though they heard appeals only in civil matters. Some blending of jurisdiction occurred between the governor's courts and the *alcaldes ordinarios*.[45]

Provisions made after the initial judicial settlement rounded out the Spanish superior court system. In January 1771 the crown created, at O'Reilly's request, a superior court of appeals in Havana designed to hear cases originating in Louisiana. In Havana the captain-general served with the attorney of the Royal Treasury and the judge advocates of the navy and the army on the court of appeals. It reviewed Louisiana court decisions in cases involving sums over 330 pesos and in a variety of criminal matters. For instance, the Cuban court heard appeals in all death penalty cases. Because of the expense, civil cases rarely made it to Havana for appeal.[46] Between 1800 and 1802 the crown transferred all appellate actions to the *audiencia* at Puerto Príncipe.[47]

In Louisiana the cabildo also heard minor appeals in cases involving amounts less than 330 pesos. Two *regidores* heard the appeal along with the original judge. Their decisions went to Havana on appeal. Spanish procedure restricted cabildo appeals to matters of law, but some arguments on facts apparently took place.[48]

43. Din and Harkins, *New Orleans Cabildo,* 103–5.

44. Din and Harkins point out that these courts have been the source of much confusion because historians have translated the term *ordinario* to mean "petty." It would be incorrect to refer to these tribunals as "petty courts" as they served more as superior courts for those "who did not possess a *fuero*." Ibid., 105.

45. Ibid., 105–7.

46. Ibid., 117.

47. Ibid., 116.

48. Ibid., 118.

These courts formed the basis of Louisiana's superior court system under the Spanish regime. In addition, an inferior court system also flourished. O'Reilly divided the province into eleven districts under military commanders, and vested each with nominal civil and criminal jurisdiction. In these districts the post commander, district syndic, and *alcalde de barrio* all possessed a measure of judicial discretion. These officers heard ordinary causes such as petty criminal cases, small lawsuits, and probate actions.[49] In the districts the Spanish officials, especially the district syndics, blended their judicial activities with administrative tasks, functioning much like the justices of the peace in the neighboring British North American colonies.

Generally, O'Reilly's measures proved sound. He induced the Spanish government to recognize French land grants, soothing any lingering fears of confiscation among the citizenry. The new courts functioned well and soon won the trust of the French inhabitants. Cabildo officials dispensed Spanish justice with prudence and good will. Often, the Spanish authorities convinced litigants to settle their differences out of court, thereby reinforcing a sense of community. As in most colonial provinces, corruption flourished under the Spanish system, but it consisted mostly of "honest graft" and aroused little significant opposition from French citizens.[50]

Although minor differences existed between French and Spanish legal tribunals, on the whole the civilian system of Castile differed little in theory from the French codes to which Louisiana's citizens had become accustomed. Accordingly, the transition from French to Spanish leadership, insofar as judicial administration was concerned, proceeded smoothly.[51]

Despite such satisfaction, storm clouds hovered on the horizon. When Laussat received the colony for Napoleon in 1803, he instituted a series of reforms that left the government, especially the judicial system, in a confused state on the eve of the American takeover. A lengthy territorial test period and an interval of vigorous activity in the first few decades of statehood would be necessary for Louisianians to flesh out an acceptable judicial and legal system.

49. Ibid., 118–20.
50. Ibid., 122–5.
51. Ibid., 125–6.

2

COURTS AND THE "CLASH OF CULTURES," 1803–1812

The Territory of Orleans

On 20 December 1803, in a crowded hallway of the Hotel de Ville, Pierre Clément de Laussat solemnly passed the keys to the City of New Orleans to W. C. C. Claiborne and James Wilkinson. The three officials then moved to the balcony of the city hall and watched as guards lowered the Tricolor to allow the Stars and Stripes to take its place. When the two flags reached the same level, a single cannon shot rang out, touching off a salute from all of the forts and batteries along the Mississippi. With those opening salvos, initially a celebration of peace and transition, the natives of Louisiana and its new American citizens engaged in a complicated battle for cultural hegemony. One of the central skirmishes of that clash centered on the legal administration of the territory.

Traditionally, historians have looked to the legislative battle over the reception of civilian precepts as the basis of the region's private law and judged the affair a "victory" for a native or Creole faction of the state's legal order.[1] This characterization of Louisiana as an anomaly in the

---

1. Samuel B. Groner, "Louisiana Law: Its Development in the First Quarter Century of American Rule," *Louisiana Law Review* 8 (January 1948): 350–82; Elizabeth Gaspar Brown, "Legal Systems in Conflict: Orleans Territory, 1804–1812," *American Journal of Legal History* 1 (1957): 35–75; Elizabeth Gaspar Brown, "Law and Government in the Louisiana Purchase: 1803–1804," *Wayne Law Review* 2 (1956): 169–89; George Dargo, *Jefferson's Louisi-*

American judicial system obscured the profound influence of Anglo-American principles on Louisiana's legal development.[2] Those precepts invaded Louisiana's legal heritage largely through the efforts of a bench and bar dominated by American lawyers and judges. The actions of those men, evident in the practices and procedures of the territorial courts, allowed for the introduction of the common law into Louisiana's legal system. Louisiana became a mixed jurisdiction, one remarkably similar to those that arose in other American states as the codification movement swept the nation in the nineteenth century. Although jurisdictional and operational difficulties plagued Louisiana's early courts, the cooperation of the bench and bar in creating the jurisdiction indicated that the clash of legal traditions was not the source of contention.

The way Louisiana's officials constructed their legal order between 1803 and 1812 revealed much about the evolution of its judicial system and the early steps in the Americanization of Louisiana. During that critical period, Louisiana's leaders created a common law judiciary to preside over a developing mixed jurisdiction. These administrative decisions allowed for a stronger measure of judicial leadership than would have been possible under a purely civilian judiciary in which judges closely adhere

---

ana: *Politics and the Clash of Legal Traditions* (Cambridge, Mass.: Harvard University Press, 1975), passim; Richard H. Kilbourne, Jr., "An Overview of the Work of the Territorial Court, 1804–1808, a Missing Chapter in the Development of the Louisiana Civil Code," in Edward F. Haas, ed., *Louisiana's Legal Heritage* (Pensacola, Fla.: Perdido Bay Press, 1983), 107–9; Richard H. Kilbourne, Jr., *A History of the Louisiana Civil Code: The Formative Years, 1803–1839* (Baton Rouge: Louisiana State University Press, 1987), passim.

2. There are numerous instances of this interpretation. For example, in a work intended to introduce lay persons to the American legal system, Lawrence M. Friedman commented on Louisiana's lack of a common law tradition; see *American Law: An Introduction* (New York: W. W. Norton, 1984), 44. Perhaps the most significant example is Charles Cook's decision not to include Louisiana in his monumental study of codification in America, *The American Codification Movement: A Study in Antebellum Legal Reform* (Westport, Conn.: Greenwood Press, 1981). Thus, the example of the mixing of civilian and common law traditions in American jurisdictions, first evident in Louisiana, has been ignored. Cook viewed Louisiana as unusual because of its civilian heritage. But when one views the development of private law in nineteenth-century United States courts, the solutions to the problem of mingling the two systems, first fleshed out in Louisiana, appear to be remarkably similar.

to codes and use precedent in only the most restrictive manner (see Appendix). Establishment of a powerful and creative bench required Louisiana's judges to follow American procedures. They injected Anglo-American legal traditions into Louisiana's jurisprudence easily because the common law practice of *stare decisis* allowed for judge-made law, a phenomenon alien to the civil law. The very structure and complexion of the judiciary increased the influence of Anglo-American patterns of judicature on Louisiana's judicial system.

Evolution of the American-style mixed jurisdiction in Louisiana began when Prefect Laussat arrived in New Orleans. Laussat possessed all of the talents of an imperial bureaucrat. Earning his stripes in the tropics, he looked forward to the passage of Louisiana to France following the Treaty of San Ildefonso in 1800. He convinced Napoleon to appoint him governor of the colony. But before Laussat could reach Louisiana, Bonaparte negotiated its sale to the United States. The proconsul then changed Laussat's instructions from assuming the role of governor to presiding over the retrocession of the colony from Spain and effecting cession of the territory to Wilkinson and Claiborne. In fact, the proconsul intended for the two acts to occur on the same day. Contrary to Napoleon's designs, however, Wilkinson and Claiborne could not reach New Orleans in time to allow the plan to take place, forcing Laussat to preside over the colony for three weeks.

Although Laussat's instructions reflected Napoleon's thinking, the prefect inexplicably embarked on an effort to restructure the colony's government. One of his first steps was to suspend the Spanish laws and the cabildo. Before Laussat could erect a French court to take the cabildo's place, however, he turned Louisiana over to the Americans. Accordingly, the Americans received a territory without courts or laws, and with a citizenry clamoring for a means to resolve their mounting legal disputes.[3]

Laussat dissolved the cabildo either to pursue his own foreign policy or to engage in a secret Napoleonic plot to cause confusion and revolt in Louisiana when the Americans took possession of the territory. Since

3. Dargo, *Jefferson's Louisiana*, 105.

Laussat was a proud man who had looked forward to his position in Louisiana, one doubts that his administrative shenanigans reflected his own designs on the colony.[4] No evidence exists, however, to give credence to the theory that he engaged in a clandestine attempt with the proconsul to create confusion in Louisiana and to foil the American takeover. Nonetheless, Laussat's actions created significant difficulties for the territory's new guardians. As in the case of the Spanish takeover, Louisianians viewed the new government with skepticism. The same fears of dispossession resulting from alien land policies reared their heads among the *ancienne population*. Laussat's suspension of the cabildo, moreover, exacerbated the situation by paralyzing the colony's administrative procedures. Whatever his motives were, Laussat's actions destabilized the colony on the eve of the American takeover. Such instability was all too familiar and its dangers far too evident to all concerned. In 1766, Charles III had assumed leadership of a region that had benefitted from some form of civilian government, and still the residents rebelled.

Laussat's actions presented Jefferson, Wilkinson, and Claiborne with a serious administrative problem. Suspension of the cabildo effectively erased all governmental and judicial direction in the territory. When this civil paralysis was combined with the suspicions and anxieties of the native citizenry, the Americans' tasks became all too dangerous. To govern the territory, the United States would have to reconstruct government from the ground up.

In view of such instability, President Jefferson and Congress swiftly adopted measures to bring order to the Purchase. On 26 March 1804 Congress divided the territory into two units. Orleans Territory, comprising most of present-day Louisiana, promised to be the most difficult to govern. Its long-settled port and ethnic hodgepodge of historically troublesome residents would require prudent, even inspired leadership in order to effect a smooth transition. To manage the province, Congress provided for a system of conciliar government, with a governor and a thirteen-man

4. E. Wilson Lyon, *Louisiana in French Diplomacy, 1759–1804* (Norman: University of Oklahoma Press, 1934), 243–6.

legislative council at the head.[5] Judging that the Creole population of the territory would be suspicious of rash innovation and brusque leadership, Jefferson appointed Claiborne, a cautious politician with experience in frontier government, as governor.[6]

Unlike Ulloa, Claiborne boasted considerable talents that qualified him for the job. A politician, not a soldier, Claiborne had served a lengthy apprenticeship before he assumed a leadership role. At fifteen he accepted a post as clerk of the United States House of Representatives. Six years later, he returned home to Sussex, Virginia, to read law. His education complete, Claiborne, like many young Virginians of his day, sought his fortune on the Tennessee frontier. There he established a thriving criminal practice and rose quickly through the ranks of the frontier elite. In 1796 when Tennessee petitioned for statehood, Claiborne became a delegate to the territorial constitutional convention. He topped off that service with an appointment to the state supreme court in the same year and from there went on to sit in the United States House of Representatives when Andrew Jackson resigned in 1797 to pursue a Senate post. These early achievements drew notice from his cousin, President Jefferson, who appointed Claiborne governor of Mississippi. When Jefferson purchased Louisiana, he called on his territorial officials for advice on administering the new acquisition. Claiborne's suggestions to Jefferson on the Louisiana question and his prudent direction of Mississippi's Indian territory prompted the Sage of Monticello to offer him the Louisiana position when James Monroe turned it down.[7]

5. "An Act Erecting Louisiana into Two Territories, and Providing for the Temporary Government Thereof, March 26, 1804," United States Congress, *Statutes at Large*, comp. Richard Peters (Boston: Little and Brown, 1845), 322.

6. *Dictionary of American Biography*, s.v. "Claiborne, W. C. C."; Joseph T. Hatfield, *William Claiborne: Jeffersonian Centurion in the American Southwest* (Lafayette: Center For Louisiana Studies, 1976), 28–95; W. C. C. Claiborne to Thomas Jefferson, 5 October 1804, Clarence E. Carter, comp., *The Territorial Papers of the United States*, vol. 9 (Washington, D.C.: U.S. Government Printing Office, 1940), 307; Brown, "Legal Systems in Conflict," 41–2.

7. *Dictionary of American Biography*, s.v. "Claiborne, W. C. C."; Claiborne to Jefferson, 5 October 1805, in Carter, *Territorial Papers*, 9: 307; Robert V. Remini, *Andrew Jackson* (New York: Harper & Row, 1966), 38.

Both Jefferson and his governor wished for a quick introduction of the common law as the basis for the territory's legal system, yet both suspected that such a step would foment dissent among the territory's Creole residents. Anglo-American traditions of judicial administration did not provide for such vigorous change.[8] Accordingly, Jefferson and Claiborne moved to construct a judiciary that would meet the pressing needs of the community, to ensure American constitutional guarantees, and to allow for a judicious intermingling of American and civilian legal principles.

Claiborne's first attempt to construct a court system reflected the cautious nature of his early administration. Almost immediately, Claiborne created courts to settle the rising number of suits that had been accumulating since Laussat had suspended the cabildo. To deal with minor civil causes, Claiborne instituted a nine-man court of pleas.[9] He appointed Anthony Argotte, Beverley Chew, Benjamin Morgan, William Kenner, Paul Lanusse, Francis M. Guerin, Gaspard Debuys, William Garland, and Eugene Dorsière as the court's judges. On 10 January 1804 the court convened for the first time and adopted fifteen rules to govern its procedure. Adhering to American practices, the judges required all suits to commence by writs of summons, capias, or attachment and prescribed the form and manner of issue for the writs. Article four of the rules ordered

---

8. British officials likewise adhered to the common law emphasis on custom and usage when they allowed French residents of the Canadian and western provinces to hold on to their laws in force under provisions of the Quebec Act of 1774. See Clarence E. Carter, "The Office of Commander in Chief: A Phase of Imperial Unity on the Eve of the Revolution," in Richard B. Morris, ed., *The Era of the American Revolution: Studies Inscribed to Evarts Boutell Greene* (New York: Columbia University Press), 183.

9. The court of pleas had jurisdiction in matters involving damages under $3,000. William C. C. Claiborne, "An Ordinance to Aid in the Administration of Justice," 30 December 1803, in Dunbar S. Rowland, ed., *Official Letterbooks of W. C. C. Claiborne, 1801–1806*, vol. 1 (Jackson: Mississippi State Department of Archives and History, 1917), 317–9. For a more comprehensive treatment of the court of pleas, see Mark F. Fernandez, "Local Justice in the Territory of Orleans: W. C. C. Claiborne's Courts, Judges, and Justices of the Peace," in Warren M. Billings and Mark F. Fernandez, eds., *A Law unto Itself? Essays in the New Louisiana Legal History* (Baton Rouge: Louisiana State University Press, 2001); and Mark F. Fernandez, "Rules of the Courts of the Territory of Orleans," *Louisiana History* 38 (winter 1997): 63–73.

that "the court will proceed to trial immediately," thus guaranteeing defendants their constitutional right to a speedy trial. After describing the proper manner in which litigants should respond to the writs, the justices focused on the structural matters necessary to govern trials in the court. They entitled all parties to issue subpoenas, ascribed the liability of court costs to the losing party, and instructed the clerks, constables, and sheriffs on the proper manner of processing and executing judgments. Finally, the judges defined the offices that made up the court's staff. The judges would appoint a crier; each municipality within the city would provide a constable; and they empowered the clerk of court, Etienne Mazureau, to administer all oaths.[10]

Louisiana's citizens responded to the court of pleas enthusiastically, and soon the dockets became clogged. Averaging five hundred cases per year, the court quickly became the territory's busiest tribunal. In doing so, the court of pleas represented the first successful extension of Anglo-American judicial practices to Louisiana and forecasted one of the most powerful aspects of Louisiana's legal settlement—the introduction of common law forms and procedures as the basis for the region's legal discourse.[11]

In addition to the court of pleas, Claiborne set up the Governor's Court to handle major civil actions, appeals from the court of pleas in cases involving amounts over $500, and criminal appeals in capital cases. Finally, he took steps to develop a county court system to decide original civil and criminal complaints. These county courts evolved slowly throughout the territorial period.[12]

Claiborne, however, realized the inadequacy of these tribunals. County courts went unmanned for want of competent magistrates. Cases poured into the court of pleas. The most vexing problem, in Claiborne's

10. Court of Pleas for the Territory of Orleans, *Minute Book*, MS City Archives, New Orleans Public Library, Louisiana Division, 1; Fernandez, "Rules of the Courts," 63–73.

11. Court of Pleas, *Minute Book*, passim.

12. William C. C. Claiborne, "Ordinance to Aid in the Administration of Justice," 1: 317–9; Groner, "Louisiana Law," 358–61. On the matter of the county appointments, Claiborne's letters chronicle a long and difficult process, see Fernandez, "Local Justice."

opinion, stemmed from the lack of an efficient appellate system. An accomplished lawyer, Claiborne nonetheless worried not only that his duties on the Governor's Court conflicted with his busy schedule, but also that his inexpert knowledge of civil law impeded his ability to dispense justice, and he despaired of capital cases.[13]

Louisiana's residents also grasped the weaknesses of the arrangement. One of the provisions of the cession treaty of 1803 mentioned that "the inhabitants of the ceded territory shall be incorporated in the Union of the United States, and admitted as soon as possible, according to the principles of the Constitution of the United States, to the enjoyment of all the rights, advantages, and immunities, of citizens of the United States."[14] When the act of 26 March created a territorial arrangement that limited the "rights, advantages, and immunities" of the territory's citizens, opposition to the government mobilized.

The controversy hinged on a provision in the Breckinridge Act of 26 March that placed an embargo on slave importation. Only slaves from foreign ports who were brought into the United States after 1 May 1798 could enter the territory. Furthermore, the act granted entry only to the slaves brought by United States citizens "removing into said territory for actual settlement." Since the slave embargo directly contradicted article 1, section 9, of the Constitution, which prohibited restrictions on the slave trade until 1808, dissenters rightly contended that they were being denied their constitutional rights.[15]

In the spring of 1804 a group of Creoles and Orleans natives led by Americans Edward Livingston, Daniel Clark, and Evan Jones presented

13. W. C. C. Claiborne to Robert Smith, 18 March 1811, in Rowland, *Official Letter-books*, 5: 183–4; Claiborne to James Madison, 15 June 1806, ibid., 3: 331; Claiborne to Thomas Jefferson, 17 June 1806, ibid., 333–5; Claiborne to Madison, 9 June 1804, ibid., 2: 197–9; Claiborne to Madison, 13 February 1804, ibid., 1: 371–3.

14. Dargo, *Jefferson's Louisiana*, 30.

15. Ibid., 30–2; "An Act Erecting Louisiana . . . ," *United States Statutes at Large*, 322; "The Constitution of the United States of America—1789," in Francis Newton Thorpe, ed., *The Federal and State Constitutions, Colonial Charters, and Organic Laws of the States, Territories, and Colonies Now or Heretofore Forming the United States of America*, vol. 1 (Washington, D.C.: U.S. Government Printing Office, 1909), 22.

a memorial to Congress protesting Claiborne's management of the territory and petitioning for statehood. The petitioners hoped to control efforts to admit Louisiana into the Union, and to undermine Claiborne's efforts to create a mixed jurisdiction by securing civilian traditions.[16] They listed the slave embargo, Claiborne's "inadequacy," and the "extensive powers of the governor's office" in the memorial and criticized the judicial system that Claiborne had created.[17]

Jefferson, the Congress, and Claiborne himself questioned the abilities of Louisianians to govern themselves within the republican system.[18] Consequently, all that the memorialists could gain was permission to organize a territorial government under the provisions of the Northwest Ordinance of 1787. The ordinance mandated the implementation of the common law; however, it allowed localities to observe the recognized "laws in force" of their regions.[19] Under these restrictions the Louisianians quickly established a new government. Claiborne remained as governor, but an elected assembly replaced the legislative council. To handle legal disputes, the new legislature created a three-man superior court to decide both original and appellate proceedings. The Northwest Ordinance required such new courts to base their judgments on the laws in force of the region.[20] The framers of the Northwest Ordinance, however, did not anticipate the takeover of such alien jurisdictions as Louisiana. This loose stricture of adhering to laws in force presented unique problems to Louisianians. Since Laussat's suspension of the cabildo had cast doubt on what the existing laws were, the legislature set out immedi

16. Warren M. Billings, "From This Seed: The Louisiana Constitution of 1812," in Warren M. Billings and Edward F. Haas, eds., *In Search of Fundamental Law: Louisiana's Constitutions, 1812–1974* (Lafayette: University of Southwestern Louisiana, 1993), 8.

17. Dargo, *Jefferson's Louisiana*, 32.

18. For congressional attitudes toward Louisiana, see Winthrop D. Jordan, *White over Black: American Attitudes toward the Negro, 1550–1812* (Chapel Hill: University of North Carolina Press, 1968; reprint, New York: W. W. Norton, 1997), 389; Dargo, *Jefferson's Louisiana*, 29.

19. *United States Statutes at Large*, 322; cf. Dargo, *Jefferson's Louisiana*, 128–9.

20. Ironically, the Northwest Ordinance also prohibited slavery, but Congress provided a loophole for the Louisianians. *United States Statutes at Large*, 322; cf. Dargo, *Jefferson's Louisiana*, 128–9.

ately to define them. Claiborne welcomed this initiative since his own experience as territorial judge demonstrated the need for such clarification.

As these efforts proceeded, Jefferson and the State Department undertook the tedious task of filling judicial positions in the territory, a problem that would plague the court throughout its early history. Their initial choices demonstrated the desire both to create a common law jurisdiction and to appease Creole inhabitants who feared wholesale intrusions of common law. John Prevost of New York, Pierre Etienne Duponceau of Pennsylvania, and Ephraim Kirby of Connecticut received the first appointments. Prevost spoke both French and Spanish fluently, a talent that made him an indispensable choice for the job. Duponceau, a member of the bar of the Supreme Court of Pennsylvania, was an accomplished common lawyer (and totally Americanized; Philadelphians knew him as Peter Stephen Duponceau),[21] but his French background would allay fears among the Creole community. Ephraim Kirby, an ardent republican and supporter of the Louisiana Purchase, had established a reputation as one of the nation's first law reporters, but more importantly, like Jefferson, he was an early advocate of codification. Although Prevost was the only one of this triumvirate to claim his commission—Kirby died en route to New Orleans and Duponceau declined the post—their selection revealed the president's inclination toward implementing American legal reforms in a cautious and compromising fashion.[22] The American judicial system had to be represented, but Jefferson sought to do so by appointing judges who, though thoroughly Americanized, would be both appealing and sympathetic to the wishes of the territory's native inhabitants.

Prevost was the single most important figure in Louisiana's early judicial development. Since territorial judges made only $2,000 per year, nu-

---

21. Conway Robinson to Samuel Jaudon, 14 July 1836, Conway Robinson Papers, Virginia Historical Society.

22. Henry Plauché Dart, "The History of the Supreme Court of Louisiana," *Louisiana Annual Reports*, vol. 133 (St. Paul, Minn.: West Publishing, 1914), xxxiii; *Dictionary of American Biography*, s.v. "Kirby, Ephraim"; Eldred Simkins to Creed Taylor, 17 May 1803; and Simkins to Taylor, 1 August 1803, both in Creed Taylor Papers, Special Collections, Alderman Library, University of Virginia.

merous candidates for positions on the bench declined appointments. Consequently, Prevost, despite tremendous financial hardship, sat for two years as the territory's lone appellate magistrate.[23] During that tenure he tenaciously attacked the enormous dockets and strove to render justice in a form that would satisfy both American and Creole interests, earning the profound respect of the governor, the citizens, and most importantly, the territory's bar. On several occasions Claiborne, members of the bar, and influential New Orleanians urged officials of the United States to provide Prevost with brother justices and financial relief. Uniformly these requests praised Prevost's judicial acumen. James Brown's remarks to Samuel Smith on this matter are illustrative:

> To say that he [Prevost] has been upright in a country where the name of a Judge was formerly but a name for corruption, would, be no encomium; for thank God, altho the poor Louisianian stares at the idea of an honest judge, yet the opposite is hardly known in our happy country. . . . But the penetration and diligence which could ingraft the practice of American courts, with its *viva voce* examinations of witnesses, trial by Jury, upon the principles of the Civil Law and digest a system of practice equally acceptable to the disciple of Lord Coke and of Justinian, are the qualities more rare and better calculated to excite our applause and command our gratitude. This has been done by Judge Prevost and the proof of it is the enclosed petition signed by the entire members of a bar where the French, English, and Spanish languages are in daily use and all of which are understood by the court.

23. During his tenure as superior court judge, Prevost accumulated debts of at least $17,500. His inability to pay off his loans led to two superior court actions; see *Carrick* v. *Prevost,* Superior Court case no. 243 (1807) and *McDonogh* v. *Prevost,* Superior Court case no. 1243 (1807–1808), MSS, superior court for the Territory of Orleans, City Archives, New Orleans Public Library, Louisiana Division. Note: Dates listed for cases contained in the manuscript records of the superior court represent the approximate dates for the case. In modern court reporting, the cases are given the date of the decision. As no recorded decisions survive for the period before 1809, the approximate dates are cited here.

Despite such pleas, the administration failed to send additional aid to Prevost.[24]

Nonetheless, the Prevost court proved to be the most influential of all
of Louisiana's early courts simply because it was the first to deal with
many of the sticky issues that arose from the transfer of jurisdictions. The
most mundane example, yet important from a legal standpoint, came
from the court's authority to issue summary writs. In this manner, Prevost
directly influenced future courts by prescribing the form of the writs. The
oldest surviving writ of habeas corpus, for example, demonstrated Prevost's influence. Prevost issued the writ for a certain Mr. Wakefield, who
had been detained by Orleans County sheriff George T. Ross. His construction of the writ followed standard American forms. Hence, through
such simple actions these forms became commonplace features of Louisiana's legal discourse.[25]

Unfortunately, none of Prevost's decisions have survived.[26] Nonetheless, the records of the superior court revealed Prevost's efficiency and
competence as both a judge and judicial administrator. Faced with an unprecedented degree of jurisdictional uncertainty, Prevost ruled over many
complicated proceedings. Confusion over the laws in force compelled him
to cope with a plethora of problems caused by competing jurisdictions.
For instance, French laws such as the *Code Noir* governed the treatment
of slaves in the early years of Prevost's tenure.[27] In some cases, such as

24. W. C. C. Claiborne to Thomas Jefferson, 1 July 1804, Carter, *Territorial Papers,* 9:
247; "Petition to Congress by Lawyers of the Territory, 1805," ibid., 269; James Brown to
Thomas Jefferson, 8 January 1805, ibid., 365–6; Brown to John Breckinridge, 15 January
1805, ibid., 369; Brown to Samuel Smith, 28 November 1805, ibid., 537–9.

25. Writ of Habeas Corpus, issued 19 April 1806, Superior Court for the Territory of
Orleans, New Orleans Public Library, City Archives, Louisiana Division.

26. Indeed, one of the more frustrating problems with interpreting the legal history of
territorial Louisiana is the fact that no judicial decisions are recorded in the case files prior
to 1809, when François-Xavier Martin began reporting and publishing the court's decisions.
The pre-1809 manuscript records, therefore, are incomplete and contain only the case pleadings and judgments. Nonetheless, the pleadings and judgments that do survive offer some
insight into the workings of the court during this formative era.

27. At least until 1806 when the legislature created a new Black Code. Superior Court
for the Territory of Orleans, *Gautier* v. *Sainet,* no case no., no date, City Archives, New Orleans Public Library, Louisiana Division.

Coudrain v. *Bagneris,* Prevost heard appeals of cases decided by Spanish tribunals, which forced him to discern their methods and to rule on their judgments.[28] Finally, since he alone constituted the court, Prevost managed the entire superior court docket. Despite the many difficulties he encountered, Prevost performed admirably and provided a remarkable measure of judicial stability.

By spring 1806, Prevost realized that he could no longer manage such an enormous assignment. Inadequate compensation had placed him deeply in debt, and the tremendous workload had compromised his health. Prevost urged Secretary of State James Madison to appoint additional judges to fill the vacancies so that he could retire. Prevost's argument to Madison revealed the difficulty of his task. He pointed out that the workload was so great and the compensation so thin that "to justify the necessary sacrifices of time and feelings—On the one hand to penetrate the mysteries of a code so obsolete in practice from the corruptions of my predecessors[,] to assimiliate [sic] this to the present government without legislative aid so as to form some kind of system, to give effect to my decrees and at the same time to unite public opinion[—]has indeed proved a herculean task."[29]

In April 1806, Madison granted Prevost's request by appointing William Sprigg of Ohio and George Mathews, Jr., a Virginian recently settled in Georgia, to fill the vacancies on the bench. Although Sprigg responded quickly and without reservation to his appointment, Mathews made it clear that he was concerned about the weight of the duties and the compensation, and that he preferred to use his Orleans post as a springboard to a similar position in Mississippi.[30]

From that point on, the court's personnel remained stable until Prevost retired at the end of 1806, and Kentuckian Joshua Lewis took his place.

28. Superior Court for the Territory of Orleans, *Coudrain v. Bagneris,* no. 87 (1804–1805) City Archives, New Orleans Public Library, Louisiana Division.

29. J. B. Prevost to James Madison, 10 March 1806, in Carter, *Territorial Papers,* 9: 608.

30. Dart, "History of the Supreme Court," xxxiv; William Sprigg to James Madison, 8 April 1806; George Mathews, Jr., to James Madison, 20 April 1806; and Dominic Hall to James Madison, 23 January 1807, all in Carter, *Territorial Papers,* 9: 626, 704.

Sprigg retired in 1808, and an American resident of New Orleans, John Thompson, accepted a seat on the bench. Judge Thompson shot and fatally wounded himself in 1810 and was replaced by François-Xavier Martin, a judge on the Mississippi Superior Court.[31] Martin, the last territorial appointee, served on the superior court until the creation of the Supreme Court of Louisiana in 1813.[32] All of these jurists shared an affinity for the American judicial system. Even Martin, a transplanted Frenchmen and a civilian scholar, was completely Americanized when he accepted his appointment.

Filling positions on the municipal tribunals and the high court gave Claiborne trouble enough, but those problems paled in comparison to the task of finding suitable candidates for the county bench. Claiborne approached the job with the intention of manning the county courts with local residents who would serve as lay magistrates. This goal, however, quickly proved unrealistic. As in other parts of early nineteenth-century America, local office holding had lost its luster as a source of social status among the elite. High-born Louisianians, as their counterparts in other states, came to regard the time constraints and low pay for local judges as a burden. Political and social rivalries also foiled Claiborne's plans. Many members of the *ancienne population* followed the lead of Edward Livingston and others in protests against Claiborne. Some locals refused to accept Claiborne's appointments, whereas others resigned when political contests became heated. Some Creoles simply avoided involvement in the judiciary because they did not understand its alien Anglo-American components.[33]

31. Dart, "History of the Supreme Court," xxxiv; William Garrard to James Madison, 20 January 1812, in Carter, *Territorial Papers,* 9: 998.

32. Martin later served for many years on the Supreme Court of Louisiana. For information on his influence on the development of that body, see Mark F. Fernandez, "From Chaos to Continuity: Early Reforms of the Supreme Court of Louisiana, 1845–1852," *Louisiana History* 28 (winter 1987): 19–36.

33. Good examples of the evolution of American attitudes toward the local magistracy may be found in the analyses of Virginia's court system in Gwenda Morgan, *The Hegemony of the Law: Richmond County, Virginia, 1692–1776* (New York: Garland Publishing, 1989); A. G. Roeber, *Faithful Magistrates and Republican Lawyers: Creators of Virginia's Legal Culture, 1680–1810* (Chapel Hill: University of North Carolina Press, 1981); and F. Thornton Miller, *Juries and Judges Versus the Law: Virginia's Provincial Legal Perspective, 1783–1828* (Char-

In frustration, Claiborne wrote Secretary of State Robert Smith in 1811 that such was "the dread of these good People of Courts and Lawyers that they seem unwilling to come within their vortex, even in the character as Officers."[34] Their "dread" was understandable. Lay magistrates assumed the task of weeding through the melange of overlapping and confusing legal principles that would become the substance of Louisiana's mixed jurisdiction. The combination of American practices, low compensation, politics, and fear of the legal "vortex" forced many who did accept positions to resign in short order.

As American candidates frequently stepped in to fill judicial vacancies, they dominated the lower tribunals in the same way that Yankees took control of the higher courts.[35] In all, Claiborne made more than forty appointments to county or parish judgeships. Only four of those men—Peter B. St. Martin of St. Charles Parish, Charles De Latour of Plaquemines Parish, Michel Cantrelle from St. James Parish, and Charles Fagot of St. Bernard Parish—had Louisiana origins. All others hailed from American locales or from France.[36]

The quest to find suitable judges for the territory revealed an important aspect of the clash of cultures—Americans, not Creole Louisianians, dominated the territorial bench. Furthermore, largely through Prevost's efforts, the superior court forged a deep and lasting relationship with the bar (its strongest potential opponent) that allowed for a consistent measure of political stability within the territory's legal elite.[37]

---

lottesville, University Press of Virginia, 1994). On the battles between Claiborne and the native elites, see Dargo, *Jefferson's Louisiana*.

34. Claiborne to Robert Smith, 18 March 1811, in Rowland, *Official Letterbooks*, 5: 183–4.

35. See Claiborne to Jefferson, 15 July 1806, in Carter, *Territorial Papers*, 9: 674; for the most complete rendition of the civil list, see ibid., "A List of Civil and Military Officers," 21 April 1809, 9: 835. It should be noted here that the civil list of the period is incomplete.

36. For a more comprehensive discussion of Claiborne's efforts to fill local court vacancies, see Fernandez, "Local Justice."

37. "Petition to Congress by Lawyers of the Territory, 1805," in Carter, *Territorial Papers*, 9: 269; for a good example of the long-standing good will between the bench and the bar, see Elizabeth Gaspard, "Rise of the Louisiana Bar," *Louisiana History* 28 (spring 1987): 186–7.

Of all the problems facing the superior court, determining the laws in force proved to be the most troublesome. Prevost, and later George Mathews, ruled in favor of resolutions proclaiming Roman, French, and Spanish civil traditions as the core of Louisiana's private law in order to apply pragmatic solutions to the jurisdictional problems wrought by the loose application of the Northwest Ordinance and the lack of an official territorial code. However, rulings by Prevost and Mathews represented mere stop-gap solutions that failed to resolve the pressing need for a clear body of laws in force. As a remedy, the legislature appointed two jurisconsults, James Brown and Louis Moreau Lislet, to digest the civil laws, and it appointed Lewis Kerr to collect the criminal laws.[38]

Identifying the criminal law of the territory proved almost as difficult as defining its private laws. The Breckinridge Act, which organized Orleans Territory, required criminal law to be based on common law, but failed to provide much guidance, leaving the specific aspects of criminal procedure to the governor and territorial officials. As such, the legislature passed the Crimes Act in 1805. James Workman, an Irish lawyer, drafted most of the bills comprising the Crimes Act. In fifty-two comprehensive sections, the act defined punishable offences, established original jurisdiction for misdemeanors in the county and superior courts, and granted the superior court sole jurisdiction in capital cases and those involving prison sentences of seven years or more. Workman paid close attention to extending American guarantees of due process to the citizens of Louisiana; accordingly, sections of the Crimes Act dealt with establishing the rights of defendants to trial by jury and to face their accusers. The civil law summarily denied both privileges. Moreover, Workman introduced some extremely enlightened sections into the act that guaranteed Louisianians certain rights that would not be extended to the residents of many American states and territories until later in the century. The Crimes Act afforded Louisiana residents the benefit of counsel and "free access" to their attorneys, the right to subpoena witnesses, to "make any proof" of their

38. Dargo, *Jefferson's Louisiana*, 132; Kilbourne, *History of the Louisiana Civil Code*, 21–2.

innocence, and to receive indictments and jury lists prior to trial, the latter being subject to the "discretion of the court."[39]

As enlightened as it was, however, Workman's Crimes Act raised difficult problems for the territory. Particularly vexing was the language in section 33, which stated: "All the crimes, offences and misdemeanors . . . , Shall be taken, intended and construed, according to and in conformity with the common law of England; and that the forms of indictment, (divested however of unnecessary prolixity) the method of trial; the rules of evidence, and all other proceedings whatsoever in the prosecution of said crimes, and misdemeanors, changing what ought to be changed, shall be except as is by this act otherwise provided for, according to the said common law."

The section proved extremely problematical for Louisiana's bench and bar as well as later legal scholars. Judges and lawyers had to decide just what Workman meant by the "common law of England." Did the act sanction only those British statutes passed prior to 1805? What American criminal practices could the courts consider? What exactly "ought to be changed" regarding the rules of evidence? Who was to judge what "prolixities" should be deemed "unnecessary"? Responses to these questions arose almost immediately in Louisiana. Governor Claiborne, a lawyer himself, realized the prospective problems inherent in the legislation. Accordingly, he appointed Lewis Kerr, another Irishman and part of the governor's household, to collect the criminal laws passed by the assembly and to mine the vast quarry of Anglo-American authorities for pertinent emendations and clarifications. Kerr pursued his task as the jurisconsults compiled the civil digest.[40]

---

39. "An Act for the Punishment of Crimes and Misdemeanors, 4 May 1805," in *Acts . . . of the Legislative Council of the Territory of Orleans* (New Orleans: 1805–1811) [hereafter cited as *Orleans Acts*]; Warren M. Billings, "Origins of Criminal Law in Louisiana," *Louisiana History* 32 (winter 1991): 63–76.

40. "An Act for the Punishment of Crimes and Misdemeanors, 4 May 1805;" Billings, "Criminal Law in Louisiana," 70–1. Although Kerr's *Exposition* resolved numerous problems related to this section of the Crimes Acts, its vague wording troubled Louisiana's lawyers until 1862. For an example of antebellum difficulties with the act's interpretation, see Mark F. Fernandez, "*State v. McLean et al.*: Louisiana's First History of Criminal Law," *Louisiana History* 36 (summer 1995): 313–25.

Louisiana's private laws, as compiled in James Brown and Louis Moreau Lislet's *Digest of 1808,* emanated from a combination of Roman, French, and Spanish civilian authorities such as Justinian's *Corpus Juris Civilis;* the *Code Noir;* Domat; the French Civil Code of 1804; Pothier's *Obligations;* the *Coutumes de Paris;* the various *projets* of postrevolutionary France; the Compilation of Castile; the *Siete Partidas; Febrero Adicionado;* the *Curia Philipica;* royal ordinances; and the *Fuero Real.* The *Digest* also contained the pronouncements of great British legal commentators such as Sir William Blackstone and Sir Edward Coke, as well as various Louisiana statutes. Insofar as criminal proceedings were concerned, Kerr's *Exposition* relied on the Louisiana Crimes Act of 1805 and English commentators, especially Blackstone and Sir Matthew Hale. The *Code Napoléon* did not reach American shores until after the publication of these compilations.[41]

The compilation of the laws in force appeared in Lewis Kerr's *Exposition of the Criminal Laws for the Territory of Orleans* (1806) and in James Brown and Louis Moreau Lislet's *Digest of 1808.* With those two publications, the branches of Louisiana's government came to relative agreement about the laws in force.[42]

Neither the *Digest* nor the *Exposition* presented Louisiana with a full-blown law code. Accordingly, the superior court judges did not view the *Digest* as such, and neither document was invested with the authority of a code. When the judges referred to the *Digest of 1808* or to Kerr's *Exposition,* as they did on numerous occasions in the territorial period, they did so in the same manner as they referred to Blackstone—in the same way as other American judges cited English commentaries. In doing so, they

41. The best analysis of the sources of the *Digest* is Rudolfo Batiza, "Origins of Modern Codification," *Tulane Law Review* 56 (February 1982), 584–5.

42. This project was no mean feat. Kerr had received only vague instructions regarding conformity to the common law. Brown and Moreau Lislet, however, had to plow through a morass of relevant Roman, French, Spanish, English, and American authorities to complete their compendium. Working alone and with a more finite task, Kerr presented his *Exposition* more quickly than Brown and Moreau Lislet. For more information on the *Exposition,* see Warren M. Billings, "A Neglected Treatise: Lewis Kerr's *Exposition* and the Making of Criminal Law in Louisiana," *Louisiana History* 38 (summer 1997): 261–87.

deviated from traditional civilian practice in which the jurist's main occupation consisted of applying appropriate code citations (see Appendix). Furthermore, agreement over laws in force and actual judicial practice represented two different things. Although the legislature and the court accepted civilian precepts as the core of the territory's private law, the practices and procedures of the territorial court mirrored those of other American states and possessions. By manipulating those practices and procedures, the judges of the territorial court ensured the consistent intrusion of common law doctrines into Louisiana's jurisprudence.

After Prevost resigned, the court faced continued jurisdictional problems caused by the Purchase and by Laussat's suspension of the cabildo. In ruling on the petition of Louisiana planter John F. Mericault, for example, the judges voided a mercantile agreement made between Mericault and the Spanish Royal Hacienda.[43] On three occasions the court overruled decisions of the Spanish tribunals.[44] In *Ducourneau & Wife* v. *Darensburg & Others*,[45] the court applied court costs pending before a Spanish tribunal. For the most part, the court engaged in the type of routine debt cases, criminal proceedings, and estate settlements that characterized American court proceedings. Although these causes allowed for the inclusion of common law tenets, it was the various structural measures related to the creation and operation of the court that provided the most reliable vehicle for the reception of English and American legal precepts. Use of Anglo-American forms of writs and procedures, and the impact of *stare decisis* as a means for importing judge-made law, served not only as tools for reception but also as preconditions for a legal revolution. The courts' operations confirmed the existence of this revolution.

As was generally true in the Jeffersonian era, the territorial legislators required the superior court to ride circuit. They divided Louisiana into

43. Petition of John F. Mericault, Superior Court for the Territory of Orleans case no. 1022 (1806) City Archives, MS, New Orleans Public Library, Louisiana Division.

44. *Fernandez* v. *Gravier*, Superior Court case no. 1165 (1807–1808); *Ducourneau & Wife* v. *Darensburg & Others*, Superior Court case no. 1294 (1807–1808); and *Livingston* v. *De la Rionda & Wittz*, Superior Court case no. 1994 (1809).

45. *Ducourneau & Wife* v. *Darensburg & Others*.

twelve counties and charged the judges to go on circuit from 1 June to 1 November. In 1807 the legislators amended the circuit act, carving Louisiana up into five appellate districts. The court then sat for fixed times in Donaldsonville, Pointe Coupée, Rapides, and Opelousas, with New Orleans serving as the primary seat.[46]

Originally, in the Practice Act of 10 April 1805, the legislature empowered the superior court to hear all civil and criminal appeals from the lower courts. According to the act, litigants could base their arguments on original pleadings, or they could amend their causes to entertain either new or more complete arguments. The act authorized the court to consider petitions; to mediate intercounty disputes; to render judgments in both English and French; to summon juries; to grant new trials; to conduct interrogatories; to keep dockets; to issue writs; to regulate sheriffs and coroners; to fine absent jurors and officers; to call witnesses; to appoint referees to settle complicated proceedings; to execute settlements; and to make its own rules whenever necessary provided that the court followed the strictures of English common law.[47]

As in other American jurisdictions, the legislature empowered the superior court to issue a wide variety of summary writs. Such writs were everyday features of American courts. The enabling act included common bonds of attachment and execution as well as writs of fieri facias, distringas, quo warranto, procendo, mandamus, and prohibition, "which said writs," the act stated, should "pursue the forms, and be conducted according to the rules and regulations prescribed by the common law."[48]

---

46. "An Act Providing for the Superior Court Going on Circuit," *Orleans Acts*, 3 July 1805; "An Act Supplementary to an Act Entitled 'An Act Providing for the Superior Court Going on Circuit and Establishing Courts of Inferior Jurisdiction'," *Orleans Acts*, 31 March 1807. New Orleans's district also served the new counties of St. Bernard, Plaquemines, St. Charles, and St. John.

47. "An Act Regulating the Practice of the Superior Court in Civil Causes," *Orleans Acts*, 10 April 1805. Such procedures were becoming common in the United States and represented the growing maturity and professionalism of the bar. For a good example of this in another southern state, see "Agreement between the Gentlemen Practicing at the General Court Bar," Robinson Family Papers, Virginia Historical Society.

48. "Act Regulating the Practice of the Superior Court," 10 April 1805.

In these matters the superior court's guidelines resembled those of other southern tribunals such as Virginia's supreme court, by requiring appropriate district and superior court justices to ride circuit, to entertain pleadings based on both original and amended briefs, and to issue necessary writs and executions according to the common law. The day-to-day routine and forms of pleading in the jurisdictions were essentially the same.[49]

The legislature also granted the superior court a certain measure of rule-making discretion that followed American patterns of judicial development. A need for courts to flesh out their own procedures to meet unique demands necessitated this extension of authority. Some of the early rules that the Orleans justices ordered offer important glimpses into what concerned their territorial tribunal in its formative years.

For the period between 1804 and 1809, before the court's proceedings were reported, the extant records produced only two allusions to court rules. The judgment in *Heyman* v. *Woods* refers to a court rule that allowed the judges to appoint referees to examine Woods's accounts to determine the amount of debt he owed the plaintiff. The court cited a similar rule in *Jenkins* v. *Lartique et al.* in which Joseph Faurie and Charles Patton were appointed as appraisers of the defendant's estate.[50]

On several occasions after 1809, when François-Xavier Martin began editing his *Reports,* the court engaged in rule-making sessions. In their first reported rules the judges authored important guidelines to facilitate the court's operation. Since jury trials were new to Louisiana, the first recorded court rules established procedures regarding selection of juries. These measures specified the sheriff's duties, the obligations of the litigants, and the court's own ability to issue venire writs. Next, the court

---

49. Roeber, *Faithful Magistrates,* 203–16; cf. Charles F. Hobson et al., eds., *The Papers of John Marshall,* vol. 5 (Chapel Hill: University of North Carolina Press in Association with the Institute of Early American History and Culture, 1987), xxviii–xxxiii.

50. *Heyman* v. *Woods,* Superior Court case no. 787 (1807); *Jenkins* v. *Lartique et al.,* Superior Court case no. 796 (1806–1807). In addition to these references, the only other allusion to pre-1809 rules comes from an undated tear sheet of court rules in the Edward Livingston Papers, Department of Special Collections, Firestone Library, Princeton University. For a comprehensive analysis of the territorial court rules, see Fernandez, "Rules of the Courts."

made rules governing the processes involved in appealing criminal cases. They regulated the methods of filing transcripts, recording verdicts, receiving grand jury indictments, and docketing criminal hearings. To make court sessions proceed more smoothly, the judges prescribed methods of motioning, filing suits, securing fees, taking depositions, posting trial lists, and rotating dockets. Finally, the court ordered that only American citizens could gain admission to the bar as attorneys or counselors.[51]

At the request of the bar the court's next rule-making session dealt exclusively with lawyers. Just as the early Supreme Court of the United States had done, the Orleans court divided its officers into two categories. The judges required lawyers to specify each year whether they wished to serve as attorneys or counselors. Attorneys prepared and signed pleas, took out writs and citations, filed entries and orders, summoned all witnesses, and declared all summary motions. Justices empowered counselors to examine and to correct pleadings and to argue special motions and trials. No attorney could serve as a counselor nor vice versa during the year covering the original application. The rule also barred superior court attorneys from practicing in the parish courts. As the court required attorneys to practice under the auspices of a counselor for at least two years before they could achieve the latter rank,[52] these early rules represented an embryonic exercise of the court's prerogative to govern legal education.[53] Creation of a graduated bar mirrored behavior in other states in the early national period where republican lawyers clustered in professional associations centered on high judicial institutions.[54] This growing professionalism of the American bar informed Louisiana's legal system from the very beginning of its territorial development.

51. La. Ann., 1 Mart. (o.s.), 82–7.

52. La. Ann., 1 Mart. (o.s.), 140–1.

53. Sometimes the court and the legislature collaborated to draft comprehensive regulations. For instance, in 1805 the legislature promulgated an explicit fee bill that set the standard fees attorneys and counselors could charge for their services. "An Act Establishing and Explicit Fee Bill," *Orleans Acts,* 27 April 1805.

54. In Virginia, for instance, lawyers in the district or superior court bar actually rode circuit with those tribunals. See Charles T. Cullen, "Completing the Revisal of the Laws in Post-Revolutionary Virginia," *Virginia Magazine of History and Biography* 82 (1974): 84–99.

The rules promulgated in the court's last rule-making session suggest increasing pressure on the dockets. During the 1811 fall term the court redefined its methods of filing civil causes and questioning witnesses, and provided stiff penalties for litigants seeking continuances for frivolous reasons. The court also abandoned its practice of setting up special days for hearing jury trials, summary causes, and scheduling pleadings. Finally, the court restricted the activities of members of the bar by admonishing them to annunciate their motions in a clear and orderly fashion and to police their seats after each session.[55]

These early rules paralleled practices in other American jurisdictions in the early national period. Those tribunals made rules, regulated proceedings, policed the bar according to republican standards, and grappled with burgeoning dockets. In these matters the practices of the superior court bore no resemblance to French civil courts or to the Spanish cabildo. Forms of pleading in the Orleans court, use of juries and summary writs, citing precedents, and judicial rulings based on these procedures reflected distinctively English and American judicial practices. In civilian jurisdictions judges mainly managed written appeals and applied appropriate code citations to render judgments. References to previous decisions took a backseat to the codes.[56] At the Orleans court, however, American judges met with American lawyers and decided cases according to American juridical procedures. The civilian tradition lacked such examples of judicial authority and the creative aspect of judge-made law.

The territorial period marked the beginning of a legal transformation of Louisiana—a transformation that originated and took place largely in the courts. Laussat's suspension of the cabildo and the subsequent failure to invest Louisiana with an authoritative code allowed for frequent borrowing from English and American judicial traditions. Legislative and ju-

---

55. La. Ann., 2 Mart. (o.s.), 1–10.

56. For a lively discussion of these differences in the role of the judge in present-day civil and common law jurisdictions, see Jean Baudouin, "Impact of Common Law in Louisiana and Quebec," 1–38; and Albert Tate, Jr., "The Role of the Judge in Mixed Jurisdictions: The Louisiana Experience," both in Joseph Dainow, ed., *The Role of the Judicial Decisions and Doctrine in Civil Law and Mixed Jurisdictions* (Baton Rouge: Louisiana State University Press, 1974), 1–38.

dicial restrictions on the construction of summary writs made further borrowing possible for the judges. Domination of the bar started with the territorial court's regulatory provisions in rule-making sessions—provisions promulgated at the request of Louisiana's lawyers. This deferential relationship of court over bar has existed within Louisiana's appellate structure since the very beginning of the territory's judicial history.[57]

On the cession of the colony to the United States, all of the preconditions necessary for legal change existed in Louisiana. Confusion over the laws in force had made the legal system "cumbrous and remote from social realities." The subsequent attempts to define the laws in force via the *Digest of 1808* and Kerr's *Exposition* facilitated the further introduction of Anglo-American traditions, thus allowing for the "realistic borrowing" of foreign legal principles. Although the transfer of Louisiana did not signify a social or political revolution, the rebuilding of the territory's administration according to American standards represented a change tantamount to a revolution in government. Finally, the change within the elite structure of Louisiana, stimulated by the Purchase, led many Americans to fill important governmental and judicial posts, allowing for a "forceful elite" to use "law as a tool" for legal change.

The legal and judicial changes of the territorial period led to the development of a common law-oriented juridical discourse within a mixed system of laws. With the entry of Louisiana into the Union and the calling of a constitutional convention, Louisiana's lawmakers were presented with an opportunity to comment on and revise the structure of the state's judiciary. Whether they would incorporate the pattern of courts and judicial discourse that had developed in the territorial period or revert to more orthodox civilian patterns of justice depended on the type of judiciary they would create in the constitutional revision.

57. For a good example of how this dominance continued in the antebellum period, see Gaspard, "Rise of the Louisiana Bar," 186–7.

3

ORDER AND CHAOS
Organizing the Early Supreme Court

The accommodations made for both civilian and Anglo-American legal and judicial traditions in the territorial era mirror the history of Americanization in Louisiana. In the courts, judges and lawyers, for the most part, eschewed their parochial interests in favor of a middle ground. Of course, the 1808 battle over the *Digest* inflamed patriotic sensibilities and cultural differences, but the ultimate settlement represented the logical blending of legal precepts so typical of the American judiciary of the day. These developments, however, represented only temporary territorial arrangements. Theoretically, when the Louisianians petitioned for statehood, they could have unraveled all the work of the past in favor of a strict common law or civil law scheme. But they did not. Rather, the delegates at the constitutional convention prudently used the established patterns of justice pioneered in the territorial period. The resulting early state judiciary, like its territorial predecessor, blended civilian and American conceptions of law in distinctively American courts. For President James Madison and Governor Claiborne, this must have seemed a happy convenience. For the citizens of Louisiana, the decisions mattered little, as their only concern was for stable and consistent justice. For Edward Livingston and his American cohorts who sought to pin their own political advancement on the disgruntlements of the *ancienne population,* the settlement represented a bitter pill. The competing aims of these groups shaped the task for the

supreme court's first judges, who not only had the thorny task of travers-
ing a variety of jurisdictions in their decisions, but also had to provide a
form of justice acceptable to all sides.

Louisiana's first supreme court judges, then, faced a more difficult task
than their brethren in other southern states. Unlike other jurisdictions
that built on established forms, Louisiana's high appellate courts started
almost from scratch. Although the Superior Court for the Territory of
Orleans had settled certain basic organizational and jurisdictional problems, the supreme court drew its definition from a brand new state constitution that placed additional restrictions on the judiciary. Moreover,
although the court used the model of its territorial predecessor, it still had
to define its role within the legal culture of the new state. At first the
judges followed the example of the superior court and used their rule-
making discretion to mold the court into a representative American tribunal.

The 1812 constitution provided a blueprint for the court. When the
delegates debated the judiciary article, they conformed to American practice and created a judiciary branch consistent with republican principles
of justice. What such a court would do was beyond the comprehension of
some of the delegates, especially the Creole faction. In the end, they left
the creation of the court to the legislature and to the judges themselves.
The so-called Creole-American clash of legal traditions failed to present
significant problems for the delegates. Although the initial draft of the
judiciary article drew opposition from members of the committee of the
whole for its lack of specificity and failure to protect the *ancienne population's* traditional civilian legal customs, subsequent debates in the judiciary
committee dealt with more mundane issues of the court's organization
such as the number of judges, timing of sessions, and circuit requirements.

When the debates subsided, the original judiciary article proposed a
"hierarchical" judicial system based on American institutions. Insofar as
the supreme court was concerned, the convention proposed a three-man
court that could be expanded to five members if necessary. Seeking to re-
strict the tribunal to cases of financial significance, the committee proposed a monetary floor of $300 on prospective appeals.

Actually, the proposal for the supreme court drew scant criticism from other members of the convention. The most vexing problem concerned the selection of judges. Originally, the article granted the legislature the right to appoint the judges; however, it provided no guidance regarding qualifications, terms of service, or impeachment. Creole members of the convention worried that to include such vagaries would allow the American faction in the legislature to control appointments to the judiciary, thus negating civilian influence and threatening ancient custom. These fears of the Creole faction spoke to the nature of the *Digest of 1808*. Had that work truly represented a civil code, the native residents would have had no apprehensions.

To smooth over the objections, the committee of the whole appointed a subcommittee to deal with the judiciary article. The five-man judiciary committee consisted of prominent members of both factions—Allan B. Magruder and John Watkins from the American side, Bernard Marigny and Jean Noel Destrehan of the Orleans faction, and the Irishman Alexander Porter, whose role was to serve as mediator and swing man. If the committee experienced heated debates over items in the judiciary act, both sides of the political arena would be well represented. Apparently, no such disputes developed. The delegates realized that an American-style judicial system was a prerequisite to statehood. Although a few disagreements emerged in the convention, conversations on the basic structure of the court did not provoke controversy.[1]

One conflict was so pronounced that on 30 December 1812, Destrehan managed to have the majority recommendations tabled to allow the minority to present its opinions to the committee of the whole. Destrehan's objections, however, once again centered on apportionment rather than problems with the overall construction and conception of the court. The article passed rather easily with only minor emendations.[2]

The constitution ultimately created a court that represented a model of American judicial organization. The article vested judicial power in a

1. Billings, "From This Seed," 15.
2. Ibid.

three- to five-man supreme court and inferior courts.[3] It gave the supreme court appellate jurisdiction in civil disputes exceeding the sum of $300.[4] Justices would receive a salary of $5,000 annually. As in the territorial period, the legislature divided the state into judicial districts and required the judges to ride circuit. New Orleans, German Coast, Acadia, Lafourche, Iberville, and Pointe Coupée comprised the eastern district. Attakapas, Opelousas, Rapides, Concordia, Natchitoches, and Ouachita made up the western district.[5] The convention further mandated that for five years the court hold eastern sessions in New Orleans from November to July and western sessions from August to October.[6] Judges would hold office during good behavior, with impeachment powers reserved for the governor and a three-fourths confirming vote of both houses. The convention also empowered the judges of the court of appeals to appoint and remove clerks.[7]

In respect to the laws in force, the convention provided for the continuation of the system currently in place, "Provided however, that the Legislature shall never adopt any system or code of laws, by a general reference to the said system or code, but in all cases, shall specify the several provisions of the laws it may enact." Finally, the judiciary article required all of the state's judges to refer to the particular authority cited in any definitive judgment and to adduce the reasons for the judgment in a formal, written decision.[8]

3. Which branch of government should grant judicial appointments proved to be a volatile issue within the convention. As a result, the committee left the matter unresolved. Governor Claiborne assumed the authority in 1813, however, and the legislature acquiesced and approved his appointees with only minimum resistance. However, the legislators held up Pierre Derbigny's appointment for nearly a month. See Billings, "From This Seed" and Warren M. Billings, ed., *The Historic Rules of the Supreme Court of Louisiana, 1813–1879* (Lafayette: Center for Louisiana Studies, University of Southwestern Louisiana, 1985), xii.

4. Note that the monetary floor was the same as that of the Superior Court for the Territory of Orleans.

5. Thorpe, *Federal and State Constitutions*, 1386–1387. Note that the district organization roughly mirrored that of the Superior Court for the Territory of Orleans, supra, chap. 3.

6. The legislature withheld the right to change session sites every five years.

7. Thorpe, *Federal and State Constitutions*, 1388.

8. Ibid.

The convention created a model American bench. As in other southern states, judges would meet at appropriate times and in regulated districts, hear major civil appeals, regulate their own officers, and administer justice. Moreover, the clause pertaining to the laws in force guaranteed that Louisiana would remain a mixed jurisdiction.[9]

Even though Louisiana was a relative newcomer to the republican system, its first judiciary article proved to be an efficient, succinct, and representative example of American patterns of court construction. One reason for the success was that Louisiana's constitution builders were able to borrow from the experience of their counterparts in other states. Two delegates, James Brown and Allan B. Magruder, had served in Kentucky's constitutional convention.[10] Moreover, American justice in its appellate form had been operating elsewhere steadily since the American Revolution. Louisianians, too, had become relatively conversant in these forms since the days of the Purchase. The very fact that Louisianians could draw experience from other states as well as their own led to a much less complicated judiciary article and subsequent legislative acts than similar creations in other southern states. For instance, in Virginia, Jefferson's early court bills were drawn up amidst a swirl of revolution and nation building. Experimentation, haste, and much confusion over internal politics informed debates over the Old Dominion's judiciary. Moreover, the Virginians at first sought to re-create everything that was English in regard to their judiciary. They established higher courts to meet individual jurisdictional needs such as equity and admiralty as well as appeals. In Louisiana all civil appellate litigation came under the ambit of one court.[11] As for the supreme court, Louisiana was smaller and less populous than the Old Dominion, hence session provisions were simpler.

Louisianians had already explored in the Superior Court for the Territory of Orleans some of the legal landscape that would occupy the atten-

9. This may be taken as a reaffirmation that the so-called code of 1808 was never intended to be regarded as a comprehensive code.

10. Billings, "From This Seed," 13–4.

11. Unlike the Old Dominion, the Louisiana judicial system did not contain an equity court.

tion of the supreme court. Nonetheless, the superior court's explorations were fraught with jurisdictional obstacles—issues that would continue to occupy the supreme court throughout its early history.[12] When in 1813 the state legislature met for the first time, one of its first concerns was the organization and creation of the state's court system. In the Judiciary Act of 1813, Louisiana's legislature created the constitutionally mandated three-man supreme court and erected a rudimentary system of inferior courts. The act provided for monthly sessions of the supreme court. Between November and August the court would convene at the seat of the eastern appellate district in New Orleans. For the rest of the year, the court would reside at Opelousas, the seat of the western district.[13]

The Judiciary Act of 1813 vested the court with the right to "make and issue all mandates," to punish "all contempts," to preside over admissions to the bar, and to create "all needful rules."[14] Although the constitution limited the judges' power to interpret their authority, the judiciary act granted them the necessary powers to organize the court and to regulate its proceedings.[15] Power to "make and issue" mandates and to punish contempts allowed the court to act freely in the promulgation of its affairs. Rule-making power had proved necessary in clarifying the fuzzy jurisdiction of the superior court, hence the convention granted similar authority to the supreme court. Admission of attorneys was a standard feature of most American high courts. In Louisiana as in other states, consequently, the justices of the supreme court not only controlled bar exams, but also set the standards of admission. Although those standards were relatively relaxed in some places, Louisiana's judges wielded their author-

---

12. Although the compilation of the *Digest of 1808* and various judicial decisions had solved the major problems associated with interpreting the laws in force, the main jurisdictional issues confronting the superior court were still pressing when the supreme court assumed its operation.

13. *Acts Passed at the . . . of the Legislature of the State of Louisiana* (New Orleans and Donaldsonville, 1813–1840), 18–34.

14. Ibid.

15. The Judiciary Act lent a basic form to the court, one that would essentially remain in place until 1879; see Billings, *Historic Rules,* xi.

ity over the bar admissions to inject an increasingly high level of common law into the state's legal order.[16]

In reorganizing the Territory of Orleans into the State of Louisiana, the voters of the new state sought to attain a reasonable measure of stability. The first legislature drew most of its membership from the previous territorial houses, and William C. C. Claiborne remained as governor. Governor Claiborne possessed firsthand knowledge of the difficulties that the new supreme court would likely face. As a judge in the Governor's Court, Claiborne had wrestled with the all-too-difficult nuances that comprised the territory's mixed jurisdiction. During his stint as territorial governor, Claiborne became intimately aware of the need to attract competent judges and the difficulty of convincing qualified appointees to accept seats on the bench.

Claiborne therefore sought to wield all of his influence to attract qualified judges to the high bench. His initial appointments revealed the thoughtful nature of his decisions. As territorial governor Claiborne had been unsuccessful in enticing prominent American legal figures to serve on the territorial court. His failure delayed the organization of the court and forced Claiborne to draw on the tiny pool of experienced jurists in Louisiana and Mississippi Territory to fill positions on the bench. When Claiborne faced the task of appointing judges to the supreme court, he avoided such delays by limiting his search to the small group of legal luminaries already residing in Louisiana. In 1813 Dominick A. Hall, George Mathews, and Pierre Derbigny emerged as the leading candidates.[17]

Hall had served with distinction on the federal district court for the

16. E. Lee Shepard has characterized the early Virginia bar requirements as almost nonexistent. Although all of the high court judges examined applicants to the bar, usually only one judge tested the prospective lawyer, and his fellow judges accepted his conclusions; conversations with E. Lee Shepard June 1989. In a letter to his son, one Virginia supreme court justice, William H. Cabell, mentioned that he planned to examine an aspirant to the bar if the stage stopped for fifteen minutes in Charlottesville during a trip to Lewisburg. William H. Cabell to Henry Coalter Cabell, 22 April 1838, Cabell Family Papers, Virginia Historical Society.

17. Ibid.

Territory of Orleans. Indeed, his fellow jurists recognized Hall as one of the leading judges of the American southwest territory, a regard that allowed him to leave the supreme court bench only five months after his appointment for a second federal assignment.[18] George Mathews had reluctantly accepted a seat on the Superior Court for the Territory of Orleans, hoping to parlay that position into a more lucrative judgeship in Mississippi Territory. Instead, however, he became one of the more influential judges on the territorial court, writing some of the most important opinions after Prevost's resignation. During Mathews's tenure on the territorial court, he participated in the landmark decisions that interpreted the meaning of the laws in force and the impact of the *Digest of 1808*. Pierre Derbigny had been one of the territory's leading lawyers and legislators. A native of Laon, France, Derbigny had established himself as a successful lawyer and had served in various official capacities in the Territory of Orleans. Derbigny's civilian background indicated that Creole interests would be represented on the court. Moreover, Derbigny's expertise in French law and knowledge of the language stood to serve him well as a justice. Nonetheless, neither Derbigny nor any of the judges who sat on the early Louisiana supreme court were members of the *ancienne population*.[19]

When the supreme court convened for the first time on 1 March 1813, the legislature had approved only Hall's and Mathews's appointments (American members of the legislature held up Derbigny's appointment). The first session of the supreme court was merely ceremonial. Shortly thereafter the court commenced its real work. On 3 March 1813, Mathews and Hall asserted their rule-making power by commissioning François-Xavier Martin, Edward Livingston, Abraham Ellery, Etienne Mazureau, and Abner Duncan to a "Committee to draw up Rules & Regulations for the Government of the Court." Martin had distinguished himself on the Superior Court for the Territory of Orleans; consequently, his practical knowledge of Louisiana's judicial system served

18. Billings, *Historic Rules*, xii, 45.
19. In fact, a member of the *ancienne population* did not sit on the court until Zenon Lebauve assumed his seat in 1865. Billings, *Historic Rules*, 46.

him well in devising new rules. Mazureau, Livingston, Ellery, and Duncan represented the state's most able practitioners and were well equipped to draft the court's rules. Unfortunately, no copy of their report survives.[20]

Martin and his cohorts most likely modeled the court's practices and procedures on the Practice Act of 1805, as the procedures used in early case records closely resemble the forms prescribed by that statute.[21] In addition, each commissioner had mastered the rules and practices of the superior court, which they all either served on or appeared before, and the various rules governing the function of the territory's other courts. Mazureau, for instance, travailed as the clerk of the court of pleas and transcribed the rules governing its proceedings as prescribed by the judges in its first session.[22]

The disappearance of the committee's report has restricted modern scholarly analysis of the court's initial exercise of its rule-making discretion. Moreover, future rules entered the records intermittently as the need arose. A systematic rendition of the court's rules did not appear until after the tribunal was reorganized under the 1845 state constitution.[23] The existing rules, however, ordered and regulated the court during its formative period.[24]

The twenty-nine rules issued by the supreme court between 1813 and 1840 covered a variety of practical and procedural matters. However, two issues that consistently cropped up—legal briefs and bar admissions—had important effects on the development of Louisiana as a representative American jurisdiction.

In its first rule-making session following the committee's report, the court introduced a requirement for counsel on both sides of an action to

20. Ibid., xiii.

21. Ibid.

22. "An Act Regulating the Practice of the Superior Court in Civil Causes," *Orleans Acts, 1805,* 219–60; see also Fernandez, "Rules of the Courts," 63–86.

23. For an analysis of the 1845 revision, see Fernandez, "From Chaos to Continuity," 19–36.

24. Unfortunately, the surviving rules governed only the eastern district.

furnish a brief, or summary of the points of the case, at least one day in advance of a hearing.[25] Previous statutes had required parties to furnish the justices with transcripts from the original cases.[26] The court's order represents an early expression of the modern usage of the term "brief" and illustrates the advanced understanding of American innovations that Louisiana's judges brought to their court.[27]

Less than a year after the court ordered the briefs, it rescinded the regulation because it violated section 18 of the Judiciary Act of 1813, which required the parties to present full transcripts of cases along with their requests for appeal.[28] Undaunted, the court in 1821 once again introduced briefs as part of the appellate process when it required an applicant for a hearing to file with the clerk "a note of the points and authorities on which he intends to rely" at least three days before the hearing. The rule also required opposing counsel to submit a similar "note" raising the major point of its argument within three days of scheduling.[29] The purposes of this rule were twofold: The court wished to impose some strict guidelines on applications for rehearings;[30] and the judges hoped to speed up their preparation time by using the briefs as an introduction to, perhaps even a substitute for, the cumbersome lower court transcripts. This second attempt at introducing appellate briefs demonstrated the predilec-

---

25. Rule of Court, 13 May 1813, Billings, *Historic Rules,* 1; previous rules in the Superior Court for the Territory of Orleans required counsel to provide brief summaries of the points of interest of each hearing; however, the term "brief" had not yet crept into the discourse. See Fernandez, "Rules of the Courts," 73–5.

26. *Acts, 1813,* 28.

27. For an excellent analysis on the evolution of the term "brief," see Billings, *Historic Rules,* 1 n.

28. Ibid., 2.

29. Rule of Court, 23 April 1821, Billings, *Historic Rules,* 5–6.

30. In its early years of operation the Louisiana court was not faced with an overwhelming caseload. But by the 1820s, illness and resignations had encumbered the court's proceedings. Frequent demands for rehearings represented one of the more burdensome aspects of the appellate process. By restricting motions for rehearings to the points covered in the briefs, the court could limit the number of motions filed.

tion of the judges for such innovations and also indicated the court's concern with the doubling of its average per-year caseload.[31]

Lawyers quickly took advantage of the loophole in the rehearing rule by arguing new points, not mentioned in their briefs, during their hearings. To provide opposing counsel ample time to study such newly introduced authorities, the court soon drafted a rule allowing them four days to answer the new points in writing.[32]

The institution of briefs represented a useful administrative reform for the supreme court. It also represented a major step toward shaping Louisiana into a distinctively American jurisdiction. Judges introduced the state's bar to modern practices of bringing appeals, thus reinforcing a style of procedure that was becoming a vital feature of the American appellate system. The rules relating to legal briefs in Louisiana illustrate how procedural reforms in the supreme court helped to facilitate the introduction of American judicial practices.

The court employed a more direct method of instilling such practices to govern bar admissions and legal education. Just as other state legislatures had done, Louisiana's assembly charged its supreme court justices with the duty of overseeing the training and admission of new attorneys into the state bar. Because the complicated origins of Louisiana's laws required intensive study, the judges took their charge of overseeing legal education much more seriously than their brethren in other states.[33] In a series of court rules between 1813 and 1839 the supreme court created, fine-tuned, and systematized the criteria for admission to the bar. The judges ensured that Louisiana's lawyers would be trained in American legal practices, guaranteeing the further development of those traditions in the Pelican State.

In June of 1813 the court issued the first strictures governing the ad-

31. The 1820s witnessed a marked rise in the average number of cases per year before the supreme court. In the six-year period between 1813 and 1818, the court heard an average of 53.1 cases per year. Between 1819 and 1824, the court heard an average of 126.5 cases per year. See Fernandez, "From Chaos to Continuity," 19–36.

32. Rule of Court, 6 July 1821, Billings, *Historic Rules,* 7.

33. James A. Padgett, ed., "Letters of James Brown to Henry Clay, 1804–1835," *Louisiana History* 24 (1941): 1152.

mission of lawyers to the state bar. The judges rules required applicants for admission as either counselors or attorneys to certify that they had worked in the office of a practicing attorney for at least three years prior to the application, to produce a license to practice law from another American state or territory, or to document previous admission to the bar of the Territory of Orleans.[34] Under this arrangement the court not only provided strict guidelines for admission, but also continued the graduated bar of the territorial period and allowed reciprocity for advocates from other states or territories.

Two years later the judges amended the rule to include lawyers trained in American law schools. Relaxing the criteria slightly to acknowledge the value of a formal education, the court required these prospective candidates to apprentice for only two years under the direction of a local attorney. In this vein, the court's provisions reflected the great strides in legal education that were being made around the nation in the early nineteenth century and ensured that attorneys trained in other jurisdictions received a thorough introduction to Louisiana's laws and practices.[35]

In 1819 the court eased up further on its requirements by allowing applicants who could assure the court of a good classical education, even though they might not possess a college degree, to enter the bar after practicing for two years under the tutelage of a local attorney.[36] Slackening of the strictures governing bar admissions suggested that the court felt comfortable that it had solved most of the complicated problems related to its mixed jurisdiction and, more importantly, reflected the needs of a litigious population.

Two later rules governing bar admissions, however, sought to prevent unsavory characters and members of Louisiana's *ancienne population* from entering the state's legal community. In 1821 the court refused to admit

34. Rule of Court, 14 June 1813, Billings, *Historic Rules,* 2–3.
35. Rule of Court, 3 December 1816, Billings, *Historic Rules,* 3. An example of how legal education developed in Virginia during this time may be gleaned from the various entries in W. Hamilton Bryson, *Legal Education in Virginia, 1779–1979: A Biographical Approach* (Charlottesville: University Press of Virginia, 1982).
36. Rule of Court, 27 February 1819, Billings, *Historic Rules,* 4–5.

candidates "not acquainted with the legal language [English] of the state." This stricture mainly sought to eliminate French influence from the state's legal order. Also, until the 1820s the court had followed the costly practice of reporting cases in both English and French. With the judges moving more and more in the direction of American jurisprudence, restricting court pleadings to English saved the state a good penny on publishing costs. Indirectly, the rule made it more difficult for members of the *ancienne population* to enter the bar because it prohibited the use of their native tongue.[37] An 1835 rule that restricted disreputable individuals (as well as members of the *ancienne population*) from entering the bar by providing for a brief waiting period between application and admission enhanced these provisions. The delay allowed for publication of a list of candidates, thus enabling persons with objections to applicants to come forward and testify against their admission.[38]

Finally, in 1840 the court issued its most comprehensive regulations concerning admissions to the bar. These new rules also had a profound effect in shaping the course of Louisiana legal education to favor the continued reception of American legal and juridical principles. They required all candidates "Whether previously licensed in another state or not" to present evidence of United States citizenship, good moral character, and one year's residence in Louisiana.[39] This portion merely refined the requirements promulgated in previous regulations.[40]

A second section of the 1840 ruling, however, represented a landmark in the history of legal education in Louisiana; the court presented a syllabus for prospective applicants and provided for an examination on the material. The books contained in the syllabus demonstrated an effort to bring Louisiana's brand of legal instruction in line with that of other states. Accordingly, the judges required would-be attorneys to familiarize themselves with standard works of civil law (authorities that were now

37. Rule of Court, 7 May 1821, ibid., 6–7, 6 n.
38. Rule of Court, 8 December 1835, ibid., 7–8 n.
39. An exception was made on the residency requirement for attorneys licensed in other states.
40. Rule of Court, 24 November 1840, Billings, *Historic Rules,* 9–11.

gaining use in other American jurisdictions), English common law, and American treatises. Only a few civilian treatises appeared on the syllabus. The judges made few references to the *Siete Partidas,* Justinian's *Corpus Juris Civilis,* the *Code Noir,* the *Code Napoléon,* the *Coutumes de Paris,* the *projets* of postrevolutionary France, the Compilation of Castile, the *Febrero Adicionado,* the *Curia Philipica,* royal ordinances, and the *Fuero Real,* all traditionally considered cornerstones of Louisiana's jurisdiction. One might argue, although no contemporary commentators did, that these sources were included both in the *Digest of 1808* and in the civil code, but so were British treatises. The meaning here is implicitly clear—English and American authorities were becoming more important to Louisiana's legal traditions than civilian sources. Thus, in their "course of studies" the judges required prospective applicants, as a minimum requirement, to familiarize themselves with the following works: "Story on the Constitution, The general laws of the United States, Vattel's law of Nations, The Louisiana Code, The Code of Practice, The Statutes of the State, of a general nature, The Institutes of Justinian, Domat's Civil laws, Pothier's Treatise on Obligations, Blackstone's Commentaries, Kent's Commentaries, Chitty or Bayley on Bills, Starkie or Phillips [*sic*] on evidence, Russel [*sic*] on crimes, and the Jurisprudence of Louisiana as Settled by the decisions of the Supreme Court."[41]

41. Joseph Story, *Commentaries on the Constitution of the United States* (Cambridge, Mass.: Brown Shattuck, 1833); Emmerich de Vattel, *The Law of Nations, or Principles of the Law of Nature, Applied to the Conduct and Affairs of Nations and Sovereigns* (London: G. G. J. and J. Robinson, etc., 1793); *Civil Code of the State of Louisiana* (New Orleans: 1825); Wheelock S. Upton, *The Code of Practice in Civil Cases for the State of Louisiana* (New Orleans: E. Johns, 1838). The most common translations available were Thomas Cooper, trans., *The Institutes of Justinian* (Philadelphia: 1812); Jean Domat, *The Civil Laws in the Natural Order . . . ,* trans. William Strahan (London: J. Betterman for E. Bell, 1722); Robert Joseph Pothier, *A Treatise on Obligations Considered in a Moral and Legal View* (London: J. Butterworth, 1806). Most candidates would have purchased Judge Martin's 1802 New Bern translation. But Martin's association with the publication was not the sole criterion for its inclusion in the syllabus. In fact, the entire area of obligations was an element of civil law that greatly influenced American jurists in the nineteenth century. Copies of Pothier, particularly the 1801 London version, circulated widely throughout the American south and west. For a good example of this, see VanBurkleo, "Kentucky's Relief Crisis." Therefore, the inclusion of these civil law

Louisiana's judges greatly extended their prerogative to govern legal education by specifying the authorities the state's aspiring lawyers needed to master. Moreover, the high number of common law authorities included in the syllabus ensured consistent intrusion of Anglo-American traditions of law into the state's legal heritage by giving English and American sources prominence over all other studies. Inclusion of the Louisiana Code, the state's statutes, and the jurisprudence of the supreme court simply provided for the instruction of prospective attorneys in legal areas peculiar to the state of Louisiana. Similar provisions existed in many other American states. Emmerich de Vattel's *Law of Nations* played a fundamental role in influencing the revolutionaries who created the nation; therefore, it too frequently entered into American legal syllabi. Attention to Justinian, Domat, and Pothier was necessary because these civilian treatises were informing property law not only in Louisiana, but also in most other states.[42] In Louisiana these works constituted special contributions since they formed the basis of the state's land law as provided for in the territorial settlement; but their inclusion in the syllabus in no way suggested that Louisiana was exclusively a civil law jurisdiction.

Inclusion of so many English and American treatises was as significant as the decision to minimize the impact of civilian authorities. Although any nineteenth-century American jurisdiction would require its lawyers to master such influential works as Story on the Constitution, Blackstone,

---

authorities in the syllabus ironically assisted in the Americanization of the legal system by reinforcing civilian works that had become influential in American jurisdictions—Sir William Blackstone, *Commentaries on the Laws of England* (Oxford: Clarendon Press, 1766–1769); James Kent, *Commentaries on American Law* (New York: O. Halsted, 1826); Joseph Chitty, *A Practical Treatise on Bills of Exchange, Checks on Banks, Promissory Notes, Bankers Cash Notes and Bank Notes,* 1st American ed. (Philadelphia: William P. Farrand, 1809); Sir John Bayley, *Summary of the Law of Bills of Exchange, Cash Bills and Promissory Notes* (London: E. Brooke, 1789); Thomas Starkie, *A Practical Treatise on the Law of Evidence and Digest in Proofs in Civil and Criminal Proceedings* (Philadelphia: P. H. Nicklin & T. Johnson, 1832); Samuel March Phillipps, *A Treatise of the Law of Evidence* (New York: Gould, Banks, and Gould, 1816); William Oldnall Russell, *A Treatise on Crimes and Misdemeanors* (London: J. Butterworth, 1819). The list is cited in Rule of Court, 24 November 1840, Billings, *Historic Rules,* 10–1.

42. Sandra F. VanBurkleo, "Kentucky's Relief Crisis."

and Kent, the Louisiana judges' decision to include Chitty, Bayley, Starkie, Phillipps, and Russell represented a deliberate effort on the part of the justices to institute Anglo-American legal forms regarding bank notes, bills of exchange, and promissory notes; rules of evidence; and criminal strictures as part of the court's operations.[43] The syllabus closely resembled the type of reading list that judges in other American jurisdictions provided for their prospective lawyers. In fact, the syllabus closely resembled David Hoffman's 1805 *Course of Legal Study* for Maryland attorneys.[44]

Finally, the judges provided for stringent quarterly bar examinations and a board of seven examiners. The examiners—Etienne Mazureau, George Eustis, George Strawbridge, Pierre Rost, John Grymes, and Levi Pierce—were leading members of the Louisiana bar. Significantly, none of these examiners represented the state's *ancienne population*. Eustis, Strawbridge, Grymes, and Pierce were Americans; Rost and Mazureau were from France.[45] The judges denied the participation of the *ancienne population*—the portion of the population most strongly concerned with preserving the state's civilian heritage—from the training and testing of applicants to the state's bar.[46]

Other rules passed during this period governed such diverse topics as return days; opening and closing arguments; rehearings; filing costs; ex parte hearings; assignments of error; meeting dates; trial regulations; record management; and country dockets.[47] Most of these reforms were

43. Although the court had no direct original or appellate jurisdiction in criminal causes, it could hear a criminal appeal on constitutional grounds.

44. Warren M. Billings, "A 'Course of Studies': Books That Shaped Louisiana Law," in Billings and Fernandez, *A Law unto Itself?*

45. The foreign French were frequently at odds with Louisiana's Creole French and Spanish citizens.

46. Rule of Court, 24 November 1840, Billings, *Historic Rules*, 11.

47. Rule of Court, November 1813; Rule of Court, 18 January 1814; Rule of Court, 8 March 1814; Rule of Court, 11 April 1814; Rule of Court, 28 March 1816; Rule of Court, 17 February 1817; Rule of Court, 9 December 1817; Rule of Court, December 1817; Rule of Court, 11 May 1818; Rule of Court, 5 July 1821; Rule of Court, 16 January 1822; Rule of Court, 16 March 1836; Rule of Court, 11 April 1836; Rule of Court, 4 January 1837; Rule of Court, 16 January 1839; Rule of Court, 11 March 1839; Rule of Court, 23 December 1839; all ibid., 1–9.

routine in that they set the basic structural organization of the court. However, the history of judicial institutions, in Louisiana and in other jurisdictions, hinged on the more mundane, routine aspects of their operation. In Louisiana the cumulative effect of erecting these structural foundations reinforced the Anglo-American predisposition of the court's proceedings.

Although the court's rules represented an important technical aspect of its judicial development, their contribution to the creation of a representative American jurisdiction paled in comparison to the role of individual judges and their decisions. Basically, between 1813 and 1846, two senior judges dominated the Supreme Court of Louisiana.[48] From 1813 to 1836, George Mathews served as senior judge, and from 1836 to 1846, François-Xavier Martin held the position. Both the Mathews court and the Martin court reflected the personalities and spirit of their senior judges.

48. The Supreme Court of Louisiana did not have an official "chief justice" until after the constitutional reorganization of 1845 when George Eustis was appointed to the bench.

4

CREATING A COMMON LAW

Defining the court's rules and procedures was one of the most important accomplishments of the early Louisiana supreme court. Such formative action helped to establish the court as a representative Anglo-American body. In setting the court's rules and practices, the judges exercised carte blanche because both the judiciary article and subsequent legislative acts generally accepted these areas as within the court's ambit. Once the court began sitting and hearing cases, however, its Anglo-American penchant for innovation and judge-made law soon raised nettlesome problems regarding substantive aspects of the mixed jurisdiction. What civilian principles applied? What were their sources? What role did the *Digest* play in codifying Louisiana's civil law? The first court, under the leadership of George Mathews, wrestled with these questions.

The Mathews court grappled with jurisdictional problems similar to those that plagued the Superior Court for the Territory of Orleans. Although the superior court had worked out a practical settlement to the problem of interpreting Louisiana's laws in force within the context of a mixed jurisdiction, many areas of uncertainty remained. After publication of the *Digest of 1808,* the judges rendered their decisions more efficiently. Nonetheless, by the end of the territorial period Louisiana still hovered in a jurisdictional limbo—it was neither a common law nor a civil law jurisdiction but something in between, and confusion reigned, confounding efforts to render justice to a litigious citizenry. After the creation of the supreme court in 1813, in form, style, and the use of the Anglo-

American principle of *stare decisis,* however, Louisiana's judges ensured that the state would move ever closer to American patterns of justice. Their rules, procedures, and practices continued to replicate those of other states. More importantly, their interpretation of statutes, use of authorities, and jurisprudence created a common law for Louisiana.

This very process revealed an identity crisis that created problems for the supreme court in the decades before the Civil War. As the nation embraced an "Era of Good Feelings," Louisiana's statesmen still reeled from the parochial squabbles for political hegemony that had wracked the territorial period. Edward Livingston, an ambitious lawyer with ties to a corrupt New York political junto, sought to insinuate himself into the inner corridors of power in Louisiana. Although Livingston had developed one of the state's largest law practices and had served with distinction in the assembly, he had failed to assume a dominant position as a politician—a role he strongly desired. Perpetually a political outsider, Livingston allied himself with representatives of the *ancienne population* hoping to create a strong coalition of Creole politicians that could dominate state politics. During the territorial period Livingston used the jurisdictional uncertainty of the region as his chief weapon against the Claiborne administration. By portraying himself as the guardian of the civilian tradition, Livingston sought to win votes from the native population and whip up a controversy that would lead Claiborne and all of his allies and appointees to their downfall.[1]

Before the War of 1812, Livingston had achieved mild success in realizing his goals. He was instrumental in getting the jurisconsults appointed to redact the *Digest,* and he succeeded in litigating the spectacular batture case against the federal government—a case that firmly entrenched civilian traditions as the basis for the territory's property law.[2] But these were qualified successes. The *Digest* fell short of a comprehensive civil code,

---

1. Dargo, *Jefferson's Louisiana,* passim; William B. Hatcher, *Edward Livingston: Jeffersonian Republican and Jacksonian Democrat* (Baton Rouge: Louisiana State University Press, 1940); Grant Lyons, "Narrow Failure, Wider Triumph" (M.A. thesis, University of New Orleans, 1973).

2. Dargo, *Jefferson's Louisiana,* passim.

and the batture controversy, although a great personal victory for Livingston, merely reinforced already accepted theories on the matter of property rights in Louisiana.[3] Acceptance of the *Digest* reassured the native population that the Americans would respect their ancient property rights.[4] Although social and cultural tensions between Americans and the *ancienne population* remained at a high pitch, the War of 1812 gave many Creoles a firsthand glimpse of the advantages of American civil liberties.

The breakdown of the *ancienne population's* hostility toward American newcomers to Louisiana during the War of 1812 stemmed from two sources. Threat of enemy invasion and the spectacular defeat of Pakenham's invading army (a direct result of Creole and American cooperation) presented the inhabitants of Louisiana with a wealth of common interest and an opportunity for collaboration.

From a legal standpoint, the public demonstration that Louisiana's American judges, if pressed, would fight to protect the constitutional interests of both their American and Creole constituents against the arbitrary oppression of the United States Army helped to legitimate the new system of justice. In 1815, when Andrew Jackson arrived to defend New Orleans from the threat of British invasion, he antagonized the native population by arresting certain residents for fear that they might betray the city to the enemy. Old Hickory's policies demonstrated a genuine distrust of Louisianians and a profound disregard of their constitutional guarantees against arbitrary arrest and imprisonment. The Tennessean's actions might have done irreparable damage to delicate ethnic relationships within the state had it not been for the direct intervention of Dominick A. Hall, then presiding judge of the federal district court.[5]

Hall had emigrated to New Orleans from Charleston during the territorial period. Unlike Jackson, he knew that the Orleanians could be relied on during a foreign attack—after all, it was England, not France or Spain,

3. In its original organization of the territories, Congress guaranteed the *ancienne population* the rights to their properties and successions.

4. For a thorough discussion of the batture case, see Dargo, *Jefferson's Louisiana.*

5. Remini, *Andrew Jackson,* 76. For a good analysis of the habeas corpus brouhaha, see Dick M. Lester, "John Dick of New Orleans," *Louisiana History* 34 (summer 1993): 357–66.

that threatened the port. Shortly after Jackson ordered the arrests, Hall issued writs of habeas corpus for the release of the prisoners.[6]

Dominick Hall's allegiance to the Creoles brought the full weight of Jackson's wrath down on the judge. Jackson quickly refused to free the prisoners and arrested Judge Hall.[7] Although Hall failed to secure the prisoners' release and the protection of their constitutional rights, his actions soothed relations between the Americans and their Orleanian neighbors. Generals could easily trample on constitutional and human rights; in fact, such actions had foundations in ancient military traditions. Hall's attempt to protect his charges and his willingness to face Jackson's persecution for doing so won the *ancienne population* over to the belief that the judicial process of the United States of America could and would protect their interests. Judge Hall's courageous actions and the triumphant victory over the British at Chalmette battlefield eased native fears that the American residents of the state conspired to dispossess Creoles of their lands and traditions, and fostered a spirit of patriotism that cemented Louisiana's place in the Union.

Louisiana's fledgling supreme court also played a part in fostering that spirit. Under Jackson's interpretation of "strict martial law," the state's courts had suspended operation. Jackson's decision to extend the period of martial law after the British threat had subsided prevented the supreme court from going into session in January and February of 1815. By March the court had attempted to go into session. Jackson opposed the action and his attorneys filed motions to halt the proceedings. In response, François-Xavier Martin, in his first opinion delivered in the court, chastised Jackson for delegating to himself supreme authority. Martin pointed out that the authority vested in the courts by the people superseded the whims of any man, thus affirming the nature of constitutional principles as those of a "higher law." That his decision further impeded Jackson's ham-fisted rule endeared Martin to the Louisiana community and bolstered the position of the legal system as the guardian of civil rights.[8]

6. Dargo, *Jefferson's Louisiana*, 76; Lester, "John Dick of New Orleans," 361.

7. Dargo, *Jefferson's Louisiana*, 76; Lester, "John Dick of New Orleans," 361.

8. Henry Adams Bullard, "A Discourse on the Life and Character of the Honorable François-Xavier Martin, Late Senior Judge of the Supreme Court," in Warren M. Billings and Judith Kelleher Schafer, *An Uncommon Experience: Law and Judicial Institutions in Louisiana, 1803–2003* (Lafayette: Center for Louisiana Studies, 1997), 696–8.

In the aftermath of the war, then, Livingston lost his primary base of power. To resurrect his political ambitions, Livingston focused his campaign for support on the few remaining residents who were dissatisfied with the legal system. During the 1820s, Louisiana, as most jurisdictions around the nation, was swept up in a billowy tide of litigiousness. Like their counterparts in other states, Louisiana's lawyers, jurists, and lawmakers puzzled over means to make the judicial process more efficient. By the 1820s, too, the codification movement had gained momentum around the nation. Logically, Louisiana, as a bastion of civilian authority, became embroiled in the quest to codify state laws.[9]

The movement to redact a code in the early 1800s, however, had steeled most of Louisiana's judges against strict codification. If the experience of the Superior Court of the Territory of Orleans taught the judges anything, it was that in such a complicated legal milieu, judicial discretion was crucial to their ability to render decisions. An inflexible code, although embodying logic and efficiency, simply could not provide for the plethora of challenging questions that often arose before the bench. The more the judges studied the *Digest*, the less impressed they were with it. Even after the *Digest* had been presented to them, neither Louisiana's judges nor the territory's legislators invested it with the full authority of a formal code, even though past and contemporary authorities often referred to it as such. The judicial settlement developed during the territorial period and reinforced by the state constitution embraced the common law notion of *stare decisis* as the basis for judicial decisions. Accordingly, Louisiana's judges referred to the *Digest*, the 1806 *Exposition of the Criminal Laws*, various acts of the legislature, and traditional common law and civil law authorities in the same manner in which judges in other American jurisdictions used their own local and traditional resources in rendering their decisions.

Flaws in the *Digest* stemmed from its incomplete nature and an overall vagueness that made it seem insubstantial in comparison to other civilian authorities such as the various compilations of Spanish laws. Judges simply could not rely on it as an authoritative collection of the state's private

9. Cook, *American Codification Movement,* passim; Kilbourne, *History of the Louisiana Civil Code,* passim.

laws. Early state judges frequently dispensed with the *Digest* and favored solutions from other, usually Spanish, authorities. The deficiencies of the *Digest* loomed large in many cases before the Mathews court, and the judges' reliance on decisions and other authorities muddled the jurisprudence and made it difficult for them to address some of the community's most pressing legal needs in an efficient fashion. In a pivotal series of cases, the judges disregarded the *Digest* in favor of Spanish sources, creating a sort of common law basis for Louisiana's private law, a common law based on Spanish civil authorities.[10]

The supreme court's consideration of the role of the *Digest* began with *Syndics of Bermudez* v. *Ibanez & Milne*. F. X. Bermudez owned a lot in New Orleans. While out of the country, Bermudez authorized his brother-in-law, Ferdinand Ibanez, to purchase the lot, "apparently at a fixed price, but in reality" as security on an unliquidated debt that Bermudez owed to Ibanez for advances to the Bermudez family for their support in his absence, so there was no deed involved in the purchase. At the time of the sale, both parties understood that when Bermudez reimbursed Ibanez, he would either reconvey the property or sell it for Bermudez's benefit. If Bermudez failed to compensate Ibanez, then Ibanez could sell the land to satisfy the debt with any profits going to Bermudez. This arrangement resembled a civil law doctrine called an *antichresis*, something akin to a pawn on immovable property. In January 1812, however, Bermudez petitioned the superior court to force Ibanez to reconvey the property. In

10. On the role of the judiciary in this matter, see Kilbourne, *History of the Louisiana Civil Code*, passim; *Grey* v. *Laverty*, 4 Mart. (o.s.) 464–8 (1816); *Blanque* v. *Peytavin*, 4 Mart. (o.s.) 458 (1816); *Bourcier* v. *Lanusse*, 3 Mart. (o.s.) 461–3 (1815); *Lebreton* v. *Nouchet*, 3 Mart. (o.s.) 59–63 (1813). For additional consideration of the problem, see *Blake* v. *Morgan* 3 Mart. (o.s.) 375–9 (1814); *Harrad* v. *Lewis*, 3 Mart. (o.s.) 311 (1814); *Lanusse* v. *Massicot*, 3 Mart. (o.s.) 261 (1814); *Roussel* v. *DuKeylus*, 4 Mart. (o.s.) 218 (1816); *Enet* v. *His Creditors*, 4 Mart. (o.s.) 401–3 (1816–1817); *Cottin* v. *Cottin*, 5 Mart. (o.s.) 93 (1817); *Whitson* v. *Stodder*, 8 Mart. (O.S.) 95–136 (1820); *Smith* v. *Kemper*, 4 Mart. (o.s.) 409–19 (1816); *Roper's Heirs* v. *Yokum*, 3 Mart. (o.s.) 424–41 (1814); *Williamson et al.* v. *Their Creditors*, 6 Mart. (o.s.) 431–41 (1819); *Zanico* v. *Habine*, 5 Mart (o.s.) 372–5 (1818); *Knight* v. *Smith*, 3 Mart. (o.s.) 156 (1813); *Gardner* v. *Harbour*, 5 Mart. (o.s.) 408 (1818); *LeCesne* v. *Cottin*, 2 Mart. (n.s.) 475 (1824); *Syndics of Bermudez* v. *Ibanez & Milne*, 3 Mart. (o.s.) 17 (1813); *Morgan's Admins.* v. *Voorhies*, 3 Mart. (o.s.) 462 (1814).

an interlocutory decree, the superior court ordered Ibanez to file a claim with the clerk for all monies he advanced to the Bermudez family. That tribunal further appointed referees to determine the sum due Ibanez. The referees reported the debt to be approximately $6,600. Accepting the referee's report, the court gave Bermudez sixty days to pay the debt or have the lot sold. On 3 February 1813 Bermudez neglected to pay and the sheriff executed a levy on the lot, advertised it, and scheduled it for sale.[11]

Before the sale could take place, Bermudez petitioned the superior court claiming insolvency in order to receive a stay to stop the sheriff's sale. As part of the petition, he attached an inventory of his property that included the lot in question. The court denied the stay. Bermudez then petitioned for a stay in the City Court of New Orleans, a competent tribunal. The city court granted the stay and ordered a meeting of Bermudez's creditors. At the meeting, on 30 January 1813, syndics were appointed and Bermudez granted to them a *cessio bonorum*.[12] At this meeting his creditors homologated (agreed on) the proceedings, and the syndics then secured an order from city court enjoining the sheriff from selling the lot. Bermudez's syndics also sued the sheriff and Ibanez to recover possession of the lot. The process was served the next day, but the sheriff conducted the sale anyway. At the sale Bermudez's brother, Jean Baptiste Bermudez, placed the highest bid ($7,000) but could not secure a surety bond, so the sheriff refused the sale. Next day, the sheriff sold the property to a Mr. Milne for $7,000. No bill of sale, however, accompanied the sale to Milne, because the syndics opposed the transaction. Then, on 9 February 1813, the syndics received an injunction from city court against the sale. On 5 April 1813 the syndics sued in the First District Court and requested recision of the sale. In the district court proceedings, the syndics proved that Jean Baptiste Bermudez indeed had a responsible party to secure his surety bond for the first sale. Nonetheless, the district court found in favor

---

11. *Syndics of Bermudez* v. *Ibanez & Milne*, 3 Mart. (o.s.) 17–43; *Syndics of Bermudez* v. *Ibanez & Milne*, Docket 5, Supreme Court of Louisiana Collection, Department of Archives and Special Collections, Earl K. Long Library, University of New Orleans.

12. A *cessio bonorum* is a civil law device that allows an insolvent debtor to relinquish his property to his creditors. See *Black's Law Dictionary*, s.v. *"cessio bonorum."*

of Ibanez and Milne, and Bermudez's syndics appealed the case to the supreme court.[13]

Syndics of Bermudez v. *Ibanez & Milne* raised some difficult issues. Sale of the land to Ibanez muddled any consideration of the property as a security, as it was not sold at a fixed price. Nor was the arrangement specifically an *antichresis,* because the land had actually been sold to Ibanez. Further complicating the case was the fact that the original sale to Ibanez did not include a bill of sale, so he did not have a deed to the land. Higher courts had determined that Bermudez did not deserve a stay until he could sort out his finances, but a competent tribunal had indeed issued such a decree. The sheriff, however, ignored the stay and sold the property to a third party.[14]

Neither the *Digest of 1808* nor any Louisiana statutory authority had clearly provided for a stay of proceedings in such matters to protect insolvent debtors. This gap in the law complicated an already irksome situation. Spanish law, however, did provide for such relief in 4 *Febrero* book 25, which was the prevailing law of the land until the compilation of the *Digest.*[15]

The supreme court considered all of these matters in its decision. It acknowledged the ambiguities in the case, but held one point up as being of prime importance: Ibanez did not possess a deed to the disputed property. Nor could he truly hold the land as his own: The court stated that "a property which was to be sold to pay Ibanez's claim, surely could not be considered as his own property; the idea is repugnant to common sense." Since Ibanez did not own the land, what rights did he have to it? He was neither a mortgagee, nor a purchaser under claim of redemption, nor the holder of an *antichresis.* Bermudez had only his land to pledge as security. Ibanez was certainly entitled to his compensation, but what of Bermudez's insolvency?[16]

In the matter of Bermudez's insolvency, the court found in favor of

---

13. *Syndics of Bermudez* v. *Ibanez & Milne,* 3 Mart. (o.s.) 17–43.
14. Ibid.
15. Ibid.
16. Ibid.

the syndics. The judges ruled that Bermudez's bankruptcy at the time of the proceeding and the fact that a competent court had issued the stay rendered the sheriff's sale illegal and void. The court ordered the surrender of the lot to the syndics and charged them with the sale of the land. Ibanez received $6,606.75 to satisfy his claim on Bermudez, and the court authorized the syndics to divide the remainder of the profits among Bermudez's creditors as they saw fit.[17]

In this case the court followed provisions of the *Febrero*, finding them more efficient than the solutions available in the *Digest*. This application of the law under judicial process followed common law practices by employing *stare decisis*. It also chipped away at the *Digest*'s authority as a law "code" by relying on Spanish precedents.[18]

The court reinforced that precedent in *Lebreton* v. *Nouchet* in 1813.[19] A thirteen-year-old girl, Alexandrine Dufossau, swooned to the seductions of a young Mr. Le Breton. Against the wishes and without the consent of her widowed mother, Madam Nouchet, Alexandrine and young Le Breton fled to Natchez, where Le Breton maintained that they wished to establish permanent residence, and married. They eloped, so the couple had secured neither consent nor a marriage settlement from Madam Nouchet. After the wedding they returned to New Orleans, where Le Breton demanded from Nouchet his wife's portion of her father's and grandfather's estates. Madam Nouchet granted him that share in the amount of $10,685.59 as a dot (dowry) binding his estate for the restoration of the dot on dissolution of the community. During their time in New Orleans the couple purchased some community property in the form of real estate and slaves. Shortly thereafter, and before the couple ever returned to Natchez, Alexandrine died intestate and without issue. On her death, Madam Nouchet demanded repayment of the dot (plus interest from the time of Alexandrine's demise) and one-half of the community property, which she could claim under Louisiana's laws of forced heir-

17. Ibid.

18. Ibid.

19. *LeBreton* v. *Nouchet*, 3 Mart. (o.s.) 59–63 (1813); *LeBreton* v. *Nouchet*, Docket 10, Supreme Court of Louisiana Collection.

ship. Le Breton refused and Madame Nouchet sued in First District Court.[20]

In the district court case Le Breton admitted the basic facts: He and Alexandrine had married in Natchez without parental consent, and he had received the $10,000 from Madame Nouchet as she stipulated in her suit. He claimed ignorance on the restrictions on the dot. At the time of Alexandrine's death, he owned no property, having mortgaged the land and slaves for their support during the marriage. Furthermore, he argued and presented evidence in depositions from his brothers and others that he and Alexandrine had always intended to establish domicile in Natchez and that they had stayed in New Orleans only as a result of "unforeseen circumstances." His attorney, Edward Livingston, argued that Spanish laws of contracts, and the laws of the region where the contract took place and where the couple intended to settle (Mississippi), governed the case, not Louisiana's laws. The English common law provided the authority of Mississippi's inheritance and marriage laws. It gave the husband sole control of the dower and the inheritance. The district court dismissed that argument and found in favor of the plaintiff, awarding her the amount of the succession and allowing Le Breton to keep only his one-quarter marital portion. Le Breton then appealed to the supreme bench.

In the supreme court decision, the judges focused on two questions. First, were Mississippi or Louisiana laws applicable. Second, did the Spanish laws of contracts indeed cover such a situation. Foreign laws, they allowed, may be deemed applicable if "the parties really intended to be governed by those laws" and if the court in applying those laws did not prejudice its rights or the rights of its citizens. Regarding the couple's intentions to settle in Mississippi, the court agreed with Madam Nouchet's counsel, Louis Moreau Lislet, that despite the depositions to the contrary, the couple's actions indicated that they had chosen to live in New Orleans. Yet even presuming those intentions to reside in Natchez to be true, the court would then have to consider whether the application of the Mississippi laws would injure its rights or those of its citizens. In this regard, the most important rights would be those of Alexandrine as a minor

20. Ibid.

child. Her minority placed her under the special protection of Louisiana's laws and courts. Would the Mississippi laws injure her?[21]

To answer that question, the court made the following points: Mississippi law was "at war" with Louisiana's regulations on dowries and inheritance. But that problem really did not affect the case because in such circumstances the laws of nations superseded the laws of the municipalities. Accordingly, the laws of nations governed the situation rather than the municipal laws of either Mississippi or New Orleans. Under this interpretation, the courts in Mississippi, as those in Louisiana, would recognize the incapacity of the minor child to enter into a contract that compromised her inheritance. Indeed, the Louisiana judges concluded that the young girl had probably been seduced for those very purposes. Even though the Spanish laws of contracts, which Livingston cited, were in force in Louisiana, they did not govern this particular instance because those laws applied only to individuals capable of contracting. Alexandrine was incapable; therefore, no such contract existed. The court did indeed validate the appellant's claim to the marital portion, and hence, affirmed the lower court's ruling.

The supreme court's agreement that the Spanish law would have been in force in this case had Alexandrine been capable of making the contract raised important substantive issues. The Spanish law should have been superseded by the *Digest*. But as in *Syndics of Bermudez* v. *Ibanez* the judges again agreed that Spanish laws were still in force when the *Digest* was lacking, and they could be referred to at judicial discretion.[22]

Spanish law once again served as precedent in another 1813 case, *Knight* v. *Smith*. Elizabeth Knight, widow of John Browen, attempted to void his will on the grounds that it was "destitute of the formalities required by law." John A. Smith sparked the action when he obtained letters testamentary on the will. The will was upheld by the parish court, but the plaintiffs appealed to the Superior Court for the Territory of Orleans. As that court went out of existence before it could hear the case, the appeal was transferred to the First District Court, where it was heard before

21. Ibid.
22. Ibid.

a jury. Narcissus Broutin had served as notary on the will, and his actions in recording it raised the central question in the case. Smith went to Broutin to record his last will and testament, one of several approaches sanctioned by Louisiana law. Broutin, however, was not suitably fluent in English, so he had the will dictated to one of his clerks while he busied himself in another room. The clerk took notes, wrote the will, then rendered the items in the notary's book. In writing the will into the book, the clerk paraphrased from the notes rather than recording the testator's wishes verbatim. One of the witnesses who signed the will was not present during dictation and another did not subscribe to the will until a year after the reading. Finding the will legally made, the district court charged the jury to find for the defendant. The plaintiffs then appealed the case to the supreme court.[23]

The supreme court judges affirmed that although there were a variety of ways of making a will, the laws governing their enforcement required scrutiny of the most minute sort. In Louisiana the law sanctioned holographic wills, mystic (sealed) testaments, and nuncupative wills. *Knight v. Smith* dealt with a nuncupative will. Individuals who could not write for themselves relied on nuncupative wills. In Louisiana, notaries public wrote and recorded such testaments. Generally, clerks assisted in writing the wills under the supervision of the notary, but in this case, that supervision was suspect as the notary was in another room at the time of the interview. Present testimony of the witnesses ensured the accuracy of the will and was a crucial aspect of the rules that both the *Digest* and the Spanish law prescribed. Thus, the judges found in favor of the appellants. Remarkably, the judges cited the *Febrero* in *Knight v. Smith* to affirm the rules prescribed by the *Digest,* using the *Febrero* to support a precedent in Louisiana's common law.[24]

In 1815 the court once again favored Spanish precedents over the *Digest* in *Bourcier v. Lanusse.*[25] When Casimir Bourcier married Catherine

23. *Knight v. Smith* 3 Mart. (o.s.) 156–68 (1813); cf. *Knight v. Smith,* Docket 17, Supreme Court of Louisiana Collection.

24. *Knight v. Smith,* 162–8.

25. *Bourcier v. Lanusse,* 3 Mart. (o.s.) 581 (1815).

Genvieve de Lilly on 21 April 1804, she brought to the estate $4,000, a mulatto slave named Laurette, and approximately $300 in personal property. Shortly after the marriage Mrs. Bourcier received conveyance of "a negro boy" named Charly. During the marriage her husband became indebted to Paul Lanusse. To satisfy the debt, Casimir had his wife sign a document that he told her was a security to Lanusse for the debt. The document, however, turned out to be a bill of sale to Lanusse for a house and lot on Bourbon Street in the Faubourg Marigny secured by a $550 debt held by Bourcier from Charles Massicot; also part of the security were Laurette, two other mulatto slaves, Catherine and Soffia, and Catherine's two children. Upset at being lied to about the nature of the document, Mrs. Bourcier and her lawyer, Edward Livingston, petitioned the First District Court to allow her to separate her goods from her husband's and to force the sale of the property in question to recover the value of her estate from her husband, Lanusse, and Lanusse's associate Norbert Broutin. Lanusse and Broutin argued that Mrs. Bourcier provided no evidence that she was not aware of the content of the document that she signed and that she had not brought any property into the marriage. They further argued that the bill of sale was intended as a donation to Casimir's creditors, so Mrs. Bourcier did indeed sign a security for a debt. Although the jury affirmed the facts as set forth by Mrs. Bourcier and awarded her $4,000 and Laurette, the judges deemed that the other slaves were Casimir's property and that he had sold them before Catherine's application for separation. They also cited *Madam Laborte* v. *Blanque,* stating "that the tacit lien of the wife does not attach to property sold by the Husband during the coverture, and which by law he had a right to sell without the concurrence of the wife" so long as the forms and solemnities required by law supported the action. The defendants won the case.[26] Livingston and his partner, Henry Carleton, filed an appeal to the supreme court. Judge Joshua Lewis granted the appeal on 14 June 1814.

The supreme court heard the case in the 1815 May term. In the appeal

---

26. Copies of the district court proceedings in question, *Bourcier* v. *Bourcier et al.* (1813–1814), may be found in the manuscript records of the supreme court case; see *Bourcier* v. *Lanusse,* Docket 64, Supreme Court of Louisiana Collection.

Catherine prayed for relief from the sale on the grounds that it "was made without the solemnities required by law and that she was prevailed upon to sign it without being apprised [*sic*] of its contents, nor the nature of the renunciations therein purporting to have been made." Louis Moreau Lislet, attorney for the appellees, argued that there was no need to alienate the community property, because the Bourciers were married under the provisions of the *Coutumes de Paris,* which afforded husbands the rights to dispose of the coverture without the wife's consent. Although Spanish law granted similar rights to the husband, the supreme court had decided in *Treme* v. *Lanaux's Syndics*[27] that the husband's actions would not bind the wife if she renounced laws not applicable to the case. The appellees, however, argued that even if Spanish law required renunciations to bind the wife in such contracts, "the promulgation of the Civil Code[28] of this state," which provided for no restrictions on married women entering into joint obligations with their husbands, superseded Spanish law.[29]

The judges faced the complex conundrum of figuring out just what laws applied to the contract and just what protections Mrs. Bourcier deserved. Mrs. Bourcier no doubt lacked the requisite information, for she renounced a law that had no bearing on the case. On the other hand, the judges considered that her agreement in signing the document might amount to "voluntary consent" of the sale. Equity certainly favored Lanusse, but the court felt bound by strict law. "In consideration of the sort of tutelage in which married women are living and to guard them as much as possible against compulsion in the disposal of their property, the laws have established certain rules, with out observance of which their acts are not valid."[30] Her knowledge of her rights regarding her renunciation were clearly lacking in the case, according to the judges. Therefore, the protections afforded under the Spanish laws, regardless of any innova-

27. *Treme* v. *Lanaux's Syndics,* 4 Mart. (n.s.) 230 (1826).

28. Meaning the *Digest of 1808.*

29. *Bourcier* v. *Lanusse,* 3 Mart. (o.s.) 581–7 (1815); cf. *Bourcier* v. *Lanusse,* Docket 64, Supreme Court of Louisiana Collection.

30. *Bourcier* v. *Lanusse,* 581–7.

tions provided by the "civil code," would govern the case. With these reasons in mind, the judges upheld the protections provided under Spanish law over the prescriptions in the *Digest,* found for the appellants, and awarded Mrs. Bourcier $4,000 and the slave, Laurette.[31] This case provided protection of the property rights of Louisiana's women and illustrated the judges' willingness to dispense with the proscriptions the *Digest.*

In 1816 the court dealt with an extremely complicated case that epitomized the jurisdictional problems facing Louisiana tribunals. An appeal from the First District Court, *Blanque* v. *Peytavin* hinged on matters of admiralty and overlapping jurisdictions.[32]

John Blanque, a New Orleans merchant, owned the brig *James Rinker,* which was condemned on the island of Tortola in 1805. Antoine Peytavin, an officer in the firm Reynaud and Peytavin, had insured the brig. Blanque's suit sought to recover the amount of the insurance claim, which Peytavin et al. had resisted on the grounds that the property was not neutral as warranted in the agreement. This situation raised an important question of admiralty law: was "the sentence of a foreign court of admiralty, pronouncing the property captured to be enemy's property . . . conclusive evidence of that fact?" United States courts had considered that very question several times. The Supreme Court of the United States had affirmed the question conclusively in *Croudson* v. *Leonard.*[33] Peytavin and his attorney, Henry Carleton, argued that the jurisdiction should extend not only to United States courts but also to those of the individual states based on their interpretation of the laws of nations. Louis Moreau Lislet, counsel for the plaintiff, argued instead that the Supreme Court had based its decision on an English rule, "proscribed in other countries." Therefore, the decision should be confined only to those states whose laws "are not repugnant" to such proscriptions. In Louisiana, however, there were positive laws, under Spanish rule,[34] that forbade its application and, therefore, the Supreme Court decision did not apply. The state supreme court, then,

31. Ibid.; cf. *Bourcier* v. *Lanusse,* Docket 64, Supreme Court of Louisiana Collection.
32. *Blanque* v. *Peytavin,* 4 Mart. (o.s.) 458 (1816).
33. 4 Cranch 434 [2 L. Ed. 670].
34. Neither France nor Spain accepted this premise of international law.

would not consider the property as enemy property; it could affirm its neutrality and validate the warrant. In considering this question the Louisiana court upheld the supremacy of the national judiciary, stating that "the United States are one, the particular states are nothing." The court then affirmed the ruling of the First District Court. Here the court upheld the position of the Louisiana tribunal in the American judicial system, favoring the rulings of the United States Supreme Court over the positive laws of France or Spain.

Later in 1816 the court considered a tricky, related aspect of its jurisdiction in the case of *Gray v. Laverty*. The case hinged on an appeal from the First District Court in which the judges had rendered their decision for the plaintiffs without any reference to law or reason. The court declared the judgment unconstitutional under the 1812 constitution. This case upheld the notion of the constitution as a higher law over lower state tribunals.[35]

Of all the cases involving the court's role in defining its jurisdiction and creating a common law, *Cottin v. Cottin* (1817) emerged as perhaps the most significant. Judge Pierre Derbigny introduced the case in his decision in the following way: "The plaintiff's son died, leaving his wife, the defendant, in a state of pregnancy. Some weeks after, she was delivered of a child who lived a few hours and died. The question is: did this child inherit?" Roman law and the laws of some modern nations would have considered the child capable of inheritance. Louisiana's "civil code" was unclear on the subject. Spanish law, however, required that the child must live for twenty-four hours before becoming capable of inheritance. Derbigny considered the problem of mixing jurisdictions here by pointing to a peculiar situation. "[Spanish laws] which were, and have continued to be ours, were not repealed," thus creating this disparity in the legal interpretation of the child's rights to inherit. Derbigny rightly asked, "Is that law still in force among us, or is it virtually repealed by the expression used in our civil code in relation to this subject?" At the heart of the judge's question was the authority of the "civil code." Was it a code? Was

35. *Gray et al.* v. *Laverty et al.* 4 Mart. (o.s.) 463 (1816); cf. *Gray et al.* v. *Laverty et al.* Docket 83, Supreme Court of Louisiana Collection.

it a digest? He answered his own question in the opinion: "It must not be lost sight of, that our civil code is a digest of the civil laws, which were in force in this country, when it was adopted; that those laws must be considered as untouched, wherever the alterations and amendments, introduced in the digest, do not reach them; and that such parts of those laws are repealed, as are either contrary to or incompatible with the provisions of the code." Clear in Derbigny's opinion was the judicial view of the "civil code." It was a digest of existing laws in force—no more, no less! This keen assessment was then used to decide the case. According to Derbigny, under no definition could a child who lived less than the requisite twenty-four hours become capable of inheritance. The *Recopilación de Castilla* was clear on the subject; the "civil code" was less clear. Accordingly, the court reversed the judgment of the lower court in favor of the plaintiff and awarded him two-thirds of the sum of his son's estate.[36]

Edward Livingston represented the defendant in *Cottin* v. *Cottin*. When he lost the appeal, Livingston filed a lengthy motion for a rehearing, which ultimately was denied. The court had further pecked away at the authority of the code and affirmed Spanish civil laws as a basis for Louisiana's common law. Perhaps an even more significant byproduct of *Cottin* v. *Cottin* was Livingston's profound dissatisfaction with the court's increasing tendency to disregard the "code" he had fought so diligently to achieve in the territorial period. That discontent prompted Livingston and other disgruntled civil lawyers to launch a renewed effort to codify Louisiana's law, which dominated the political arena of the 1820s and spurred a colossal battle in the courts over the next two decades.

36. *Cottin* v. *Cottin*, 5 Mart. (o.s.) 93–104 (1817); *Cottin* v. *Cottin*, Docket 226, Supreme Court of Louisiana Collection.

5

THE PHOENIX
Edward Livingston and Codification in the 1820s

dward Livingston's quarrel with the emergence of a Louisiana common law hinged on a question of philosophy. As a young man, he had embraced codification as a means of providing an enlightened, consistent form of justice. Born into one of the three prevailing patrician families of eighteenth-century New York, Livingston enjoyed extraordinary advantages for a young man in revolutionary America. Private tutors oversaw his early education at Albany. While still very young, he attended a grammar school at Esopus in Ulster County until the village fell to the British in 1777. After that, he moved to a school in Hurley where he continued his studies for two more years. In 1779 he entered Nassau Hall (now Princeton University). After graduation he studied law under John Lansing. His colleagues in preparation for the bar would emerge as some of early America's most brilliant political leaders. Among his fellow students were Aaron Burr, Alexander Hamilton, and James Kent, who would become one of the United States' leading authorities on common law. Under Lansing's tutelage, Livingston developed a predisposition toward Roman law, which no doubt influenced his views on codification.[1]

When Livingston completed his legal studies and became a member

---

1. Hatcher, *Edward Livingston,* 1–10; Edward Livingston, "Autobiographical Jottings," n.d., Edward Livingston Papers [hereafter cited as ELP], Department of Special Collections, Firestone Library, Princeton University, Box 80.

of the New York bar in 1785, he immediately found himself poised for a career in politics. His older brother, Robert R. Livingston, became chancellor of the State of New York and served in the Continental Congress. Robert's patronage elevated Edward to an exalted position in New York politics. After a falling out with Alexander Hamilton in the early 1790s, the chancellor and his little brother moved into the republican camp. In 1794, Edward Livingston won election to the United States House of Representatives. It was his first successful election, but for a man just thirty years old, it meant the beginning of a long and fascinating political career.[2]

As a member of the House of Representatives, Livingston pursued his first attempt at codification. Only days after taking his seat, he revealed his frustration with the sanguinary state of the new nation's penal laws by introducing legislation to create a penal code for the United States.[3] Surprisingly liberal in its attitudes toward rehabilitation of criminals and capital punishment, Livingston's proposed legislation jibed with Thomas Jefferson's views on such matters, especially in its attack on the principle of *lex talionis* (retaliation) as a form of punishment,[4] but was ultimately too forward-looking for other members of Congress. Although the measure failed, it awakened in Livingston a passion for penal reform, a penchant toward codification, and an unrelenting hatred of the medieval nature of the common law.

In 1801, after this brief career in the legislative chamber, Livingston was appointed by President Thomas Jefferson a United States attorney for the District of New York. That same year, the New York Council of Appointment named Livingston mayor of New York City. During his tenure Livingston tried unsuccessfully to reform New York's penal system. Serving as both mayor and United States attorney proved lucrative for Living-

2. Hatcher, *Edward Livingston,* 10–55.

3. Edward Livingston, "Autobiographical Jottings," ELP, Box 80.

4. Lucius P. Deming, "Edward Livingston as a Law Reformer," Townshend Prize Oration spoken at the Yale College Commencement before the Law Department, 27 June 1877, ELP, Box 91; for Jefferson's views on *lex talionis,* see Albert Ellery Bergh, ed., *The Writings of Thomas Jefferson,* vol. 1 (Washington, D.C.: Thomas Jefferson Memorial Foundation of the United States, 1903), 64–5.

ston, but in 1803 he became embroiled in an embezzlement scandal that led him to resign in disgrace. Although the state lacked strong evidence to convict him, Livingston accepted the federal court's judgment against him because he wanted to spare an inept aide's reputation.[5] Forced to start over, Livingston traveled to New Orleans, where he quickly developed a vibrant legal practice and soon became involved in local politics.

During the territorial period Livingston fought two major battles involving civil law. In the courts he pursued the batture case, and he lobbied somewhat successfully for codification in the attempt to draft the *Digest of 1808*. These battles were not totally acrimonious. Livingston succeeded as a practitioner before the local bar, and even drafted the petition from the members of the bar in support of Judge Prevost.[6]

After 1808, as the judges of the Superior Court for the Territory of Orleans and the early Supreme Court of the State of Louisiana disregarded the *Digest* and developed a Louisiana version of common law, Livingston became increasingly frustrated with the legal practices of his adopted state. His battles with the judges proved troublesome for him. In the early years of statehood Livingston and his partners began to believe that the judges had become prejudiced against him, and he began to withdraw from active litigation. When he did argue a case, he and his cohorts believed that the judges ignored his brilliance. Such a disposition further steeled him against the common law system with its reliance on judicial opinions as opposed to codes.[7] When the opportunity arose in the 1820s, he spearheaded a second attempt to codify the state's law.

After litigating *Cottin v. Cottin*, Livingston pointed to the prevalent disregard of the 1808 *Digest* as a dangerous practice. In 1820 he won election to the state legislature, where he whipped up distrust among the *ancienne population* over the regulations requiring the use of English in official court proceedings. He also enlisted the aid of other members of the legal community, such as his law partner John Grymes and legislator Christobal de Armas, to stir up criticism against the supreme court and

5. Hatcher, *Edward Livingston;* 93–9; Livingston, "Autobiographical Jottings."
6. ELP, Box 62.
7. Henry Carleton, "Memoir of Edward Livingston," n.d., ELP, Box 91.

its use of domestic and foreign authorities in common law fashion. Livingston's early fascination with civil law dominated his thinking on such matters. His preference for codification was clear. In a report that he prepared on a professorship of legislation in Louisiana, he criticized law professors as teaching "what laws are, . . . [not] what they ought to be." In that report Livingston clarified what his notion of jurisprudence was: "Not so the lecturer on the law as it is, he not only [exposes] the rule but justifies it, exerts all the faculties of his mind to find a plausible reason in its support. Cites the seriatitiem [sic] authorities of [Ezez] Nebuchadnezzar & Cyrus Justinian to prove the justice of the [law]." Judges should expose what the law is based on the codes available to them, rather than expound on the just nature of those laws. In Livingston's opinion, judges should "discover" the law, not "make" law.[8] His view represented a civilian approach to jurisprudence alien to Anglo-American practice.

Livingston's attempt to overhaul Louisiana's legal system centered on a two-pronged plan. A new penal code would revolutionize the public law. A new civil code would replace the *Digest* with a more authoritative body of laws in force. The penal code represented Livingston's most ambitious efforts at legal reform. Hatched in his early days in Congress, the idea to reform the penal system remained a goal for Livingston throughout his sojourn in Louisiana. His first and only draft of the code perished in a fire at Livingston's house in 1824 as he was checking his revisions and notes to the printer. As one source pointed out, "By 2 O'clock [A.M.], the whole was a heap of ashes—After witnessing the destruction of his highest hopes, he returns to his apartments, where he finds his family plunged into a deep despair." But Livingston was undaunted. Reportedly, he smiled and told his family "Weep not . . . you will see it [the code] like the Phoenix, rise from its ashes, fairer than ever." The next day he returned to his labor and began rewriting the code.[9] What eventually rose from the ashes was a forward-looking document that presaged twentieth-century liberal attitudes toward crime and punishment. In the mid-1820s, Livingston sent out drafts of the code to commentators around the world. His

8. Edward Livingston, "Report on a Professorship in Legislation," n.d., ELP, Box 80.
9. Anonymous, "Notes on the Life of Edward Livingston," n.d., ELP, Box 91.

correspondents in the United States included such luminaries as Thomas Jefferson, John Adams, James Madison, and Joseph Story. Worldwide, he exchanged letters about the code with prominent legal minds such as Jeremy Bentham and a distinguished list of monarchs. Nevertheless, in Louisiana the code died in the legislature. The Empire of Guatemala, however, adopted the code, and it soon became one of the most influential pieces of legislation in nineteenth-century Latin America.[10]

Early in the 1820s, Livingston began his attack on the judicial misuse of law in Louisiana. In a circular letter to his constituents, he addressed his two-pronged strategy. The criminal laws, he argued, had become polluted through judicial process. For terminology in the criminal law "as well as for our rules of evidence, and forms of proceeding, we are referred to the Common Law of England; hence, here as well as in other parts of the Union, we felt the inconvenience of being governed by unwritten law, daily changing by the judicial decrees on which this system of jurisprudence is chiefly founded." Livingston added that the criminal laws during the territorial period were a "source of embarassment [sic] [that] arose from the undefined nature of the common law. In all cases of definition, construction, and practice, this was established as our rule; but unexplained and unamended by statute, it was in many points too barbarous and absurd to be carried into execution. In practice then, judges were forced to adopt some and reject others of its provisions, to apply statutory amendments, to modify, to enlarge, to restrain, in short to assume legislative powers." In an oblique reference to Kerr's *Exposition,* he argued that the Louisianians borrowed from the experiment that led to the 1805 code of practice to remedy the situation. He further argued that the *Digest* represented a similar success.[11]

What motivated Livingston to make these arguments? Expounding on the successes of the existing codes would have served him well in lobbying for an ever-increasing level of codification. In fact, in addition to these

10. Hatcher, *Edward Livingston;* and Grant Lyons, "Livingston and the Louisiana Criminal Codes," *Louisiana History* 15 (summer 1974): 243–72.

11. Edward Livingston, "Circular Letter to His Constituents," 1 May 1821, ELP, Box 72.

measures Livingston and his allies also convinced their fellow Louisiana legislators that only a new civil code could remedy the problems. This plea for codification, of course, was not unique. Livingston's actions mirrored those of lawmakers in other American states who were trying to limit the discretion of judges and to bring a higher measure of order to the law.[12]

In 1822 the Louisiana legislature responded to Livingston's criticism and adopted a resolution to revise the *Digest*. It created a panel of three jurisconsults—Livingston, Louis Moreau Lislet, and Pierre Derbigny—to study the situation.[13] By February 1823 the jurisconsults recommended a wholesale revision of the *Digest* and related repealing legislation. Substantively, the redactors relied heavily on Spanish precepts for the bulk of Louisiana's private laws in their new code, perhaps as a bow to the judges' preferences.

Initially, these recommendations fell on deaf ears. Livingston drafted a letter to his constituents to explain the situation. He argued that the emendations to the civil code failed to sway the legislature, partly because Livingston could not be present to lobby for its passage, and partly because the initial draft was incomplete as it did not incorporate all of Louisiana's statute law. Livingston regarded the legislature's lukewarm reception of the 1823 report as an error, and he seemed confident that sober reflection would someday "produce a reform." The failure hardly made him reticent. Livingston responded with a ringing condemnation of the common law: "Whenever a new principle is applied for its Decision and its operations on future cases it has many radical defects." Those defects "contravene[d] the spirit of all the constitutions of the different States." The evils of common law, he argued, resided in the powers granted to the judiciary: "If the judges deciding on cases were to confirm the operation of the principles they establish to that [case] alone although they should (as they [never] do) sometimes enlarge some times restrain the expression of the

---

12. Cook, *American Codification Movement,* passim; Kilbourne, *History of the Louisiana Civil Code,* 96–9.

13. *Acts . . . of the Legislature of the State of Louisiana* (New Orleans: 1812–1859) [hereafter cited as *Louisiana Acts*], vol. 20, 1822; cf. Kilbourne, *History of the Louisiana Civil Code,* 108.

law; the Evil would be [partial] it would be confined to that case and would be only an illegal decision but when they make one such decision the rule for another, when they regard it as a guide for themselves and their successors they make a law." Such judge-made law provided a "cloak" for "partiality and corruption" and an excuse for "ignorance and error." These evils, accordingly to Livingston, could be curtailed only by the institution of a comprehensive code.[14]

Eventually the exhortations of Livingston and his cohorts swayed the legislators, who adopted their proposed amendments hastily and with little debate. American members of the Louisiana assembly supported the revisal as a routine process similar to the type of practices that had been taking place in other American states. Alexander Porter, for instance, pointed out that the revision closely resembled Kentucky's law revisal.

For the most part the assembly accepted the work of the redactors. The legislators added an amendment repealing the Spanish, Roman, and French laws in force at the time of the Louisiana Purchase. They also repealed the acts of the legislative council, the Orleans territorial legislature, and the Louisiana state assembly that the redaction superseded. Finally, the legislature provided for the publication of the emendations as the *Louisiana Code of 1825*.[15]

For Livingston and his supporters the revision seemed a great success. With a comprehensive code in place the Louisiana Assembly sent a strong message to the judiciary—the practice of consulting outside authorities was at an end. In essence, it appeared as if Livingston had succeeded in pulling off a major feat—the redefinition of judicial practice from an Anglo-American common law style of decision making to a less creative civil law type of judicature.[16] But neither Livingston nor his contemporaries nor modern day critics and historians understood the power, determination, independence, and resiliency of the judges of the Supreme Court

---

14. Edward Livingston, "Draft of a Letter," c. 1823, ELP, Box 76.

15. Kilbourne, *History of the Louisiana Civil Code*, 124–30; for a detailed analysis of Kentucky's codification movement, see VanBurkleo, "Kentucky's Relief Crisis." The repealing act became Article 3521 of the *Louisiana Code*.

16. Kilbourne, *History of the Louisiana Civil Code*, 129–30.

of Louisiana to establish and to maintain Anglo-American patterns of justice.

Almost immediately, the supreme court began to reduce the *Louisiana Code* to the less authoritative stance of a digest of the laws. In a series of cases the court redefined the role of the code and attacked article 3521 (the repealing amendment) by pointing out defects in the code and employing pre-1825 remedies—remedies that often relied on foreign sources.[17] In response, the legislature sought to maintain the supremacy of the code with a new repealing statute in 1828. Again the statute repealed all foreign laws in force at the time of cession and the acts of the legislative council, the territorial legislature, and the state assembly.[18]

Although the 1825 code and its repealing legislation attempted to clarify what the legislature understood to be the laws comprising the jurisdiction, its very institution created confusion. The judges, now with over a decade of practice in the Anglo-American mode of judicature, used that confusion to maintain their judicial independence.

As it treaded in these troubled waters, the Martin court continued to grapple with important issues related to the definition of judicial power in Louisiana, especially in regard to the role of the 1825 *Louisiana Code* and the 1828 repealing statutes.[19] In defining the role of the judiciary in Louisiana's jurisprudence, no matter that came before the Martin court is of more importance than the 1839 case of *Reynolds v. Swain et al.*

In 1836, Reynolds rented a tenement on the corner of Poydras and Magazine Streets to W. W. and T. Swain for the purposes of starting an apothecary shop. Reynolds's agent and W. W. Swain agreed on a $1,500-per-year lease payable in twelve monthly installments of $125 beginning 1 November 1836. About two weeks after Swain & Co. occupied the property, Reynolds's agent presented the Swains with a written lease. When

17. Ibid., 136–9; *Erwin v. Fenwick*, 6 Mart. (n.s.) 229–32 (1827); *Pignatel v. Drouet*, 6 Mart. (n.s.) 432 (1828); *Cole's Widow v. His Executors*, 7 Mart. (n.s.) 41 (1828).

18. Kilbourne, *History of the Louisiana Civil Code*, 131–44. Kilbourne points out that some legislators felt that the 1828 statute was defective, but attempts to draft additional legislation failed. Unfortunately, the legislative journals and other historical sources for this period are too sketchy to provide a thorough analysis of the reasons behind these failures.

19. See *Gasquet v. Dimitry*, 9 La. Ann. 592 (1836).

Swain and his partner refused to sign the lease, the agent informed them that he intended to hold Swain & Co. to the terms of the verbal agreement. At the end of December, Swain & Co. vacated the premises without giving either Reynolds or his agent an explanation and refused to pay the remaining ten months' rent. The agent protested and would not receive the keys to the property from Swain. Following their discussion the agent wrote a note to Swain & Co. indicating that he still intended to hold the apothecaries to the terms of the lease.[20]

On 26 April 1837, seven months before the terms of the lease would have expired, Reynolds sued Swain & Co. in the First Judicial District of Louisiana for the rental payments that the firm had failed to pay for the period between January and April as well as the remaining rent due between 1 May and 1 October 1837. Reynolds's agent testified in the case, and both a witness and the unsigned lease corroborated his testimony. The district court judge ruled in favor of Reynolds and rendered judgment for $875, the amount due on 1 June 1837 with an additional obligation of $125 per month until the lease expired the following October.

The district judge's opinion rested on a previous decision in the Supreme Court of Louisiana, *Christy v. Casanave* (1824), which invoked a Roman convention that required tenants who abandoned a property to pay the rent for the entire term, even if the term of the lease had not yet expired.[21] Although such Roman laws had no force in Louisiana, the supreme court determined in *Christy v. Casanave* that such devices provided remedies in analogous cases. The Swains nonetheless appealed the decision in their case to the state supreme court.[22]

In appealing the decision, the Swains engaged one of Louisiana's most promising young attorneys and a resident expert in partnership law, Thomas Slidell.[23] Slidell argued two points: that neither a partnership nor

20. *Reynolds v. Swain et al.,* 13 La. Ann. 193 (1839).

21. Thus, even though the rent for the remaining months was not yet due, the tenants would be forced to pay the rent for the entire term. See *Christy v. Casanave* 2 Mart. (n.s.) 451 (1824).

22. *Reynolds v. Swain et al.,* 193.

23. Slidell would later become a justice of the Supreme Court of Louisiana and pen all majority opinions involving the laws of partnership.

its assets could be held liable for a debt or contract incurred separately on the responsibility of one of the partners; and that Reynolds filed suit prematurely since part of the rent was not due at the time of the action. On the second point Slidell sought a reversal of the district court judgment for the $375 due between August and September 1837. Slidell's second argument brought up a crucial issue—that the court had decided *Christy* v. *Casanave* in 1824, before the adoption of either the 1825 Louisiana Code or the 1828 act that repealed all civil laws not contained in the code. Since the 1825 code did not sanction the Roman remedy utilized in *Christy* v. *Casanave*, Slidell contended that the repealing act of 1828 precluded its use in *Reynolds* v. *Swain*.

Slidell's argument raised a tricky point. Since its inception in 1825 the *Louisiana Code* had not functioned as a binding code in traditional civil law fashion. Rather, the judges of the supreme court had used the *Louisiana Code* in the same manner as they had the *Digest of 1808,* as a basic reference similar to other classic authorities and judicial decisions. By viewing the code in this manner, Louisiana's judges had strengthened their judicial independence by functioning according to the practices and procedures of American courts rather than as a civil law tribunal. In this vein, Louisiana's justices decided cases according to the common law doctrine of *stare decisis.* Moreover, their interpretation of the code as a basic authority differed drastically from the manner in which civil law judges referred to their codes—the process that Livingston and the legislature had attempted to inflict on the court in 1825.[24] This method of referring to code citations that Louisiana's judges used closely paralleled the way other judges in other states employed foreign authorities.[25]

Slidell's insistence that the *Louisiana Code* and the 1828 repealing act prohibited the judges from consulting Roman law challenged those judicial practices directly. Essentially, Slidell reasoned that the passage of the 1825 code and the repealing act meant that Louisiana's judges must ad-

24. See Appendix.
25. For an example of this, see the Virginia cases *Thornton* v. *Smith* 1 Wash. 83–5 (1792); *Browne et al.* v. *Turberville et al.* 2 Call 390–409 (1800); *Baring* v. *Reeder* 1 H&M, 154–76 (1806); and *Coleman* v. *Moody* 4 H&M, 1–23 (1809).

here to the provisions of the *Louisiana Code* exclusively, and that all other authorities had no force in the state. In other words, Slidell challenged the very role of the judge in the state's judicial system—a process that had not been addressed in any of the previous cases regarding the 1825 code and its repealing statute. If the court accepted Slidell's interpretation, it would cease to function as a creative American court; judges would lose much of their intellectual independence because finite codes would replace judicial decisions and foreign authorities as the sources of their opinions.[26]

Reynolds v. *Swain et al.* challenged the very foundations of Louisiana's judicial system. The supreme court itself had to decide whether to continue to render justice according to Anglo-American patterns or revert to the type of civil law court that characterized Louisiana's colonial era. If the court cast aside Slidell's argument, the decision would represent a firm commitment to American judicial traditions; if not, the judiciary would reject American juridical patterns in favor of civilian practices.

In terms of defining the role of the judiciary in the state, *Reynolds* v. *Swain et al.* represented the single most important issue that ever came before the Martin court. Since the case appeared on the docket while Henry Adams Bullard and Henry Carleton were away, the decision in the case was rendered by Martin alone. Martin met the challenge boldly. Indeed, *Reynolds* v. *Swain et al.* represents Martin's most influential contribution to the Supreme Court of Louisiana.

Martin understood what was at stake in *Reynolds* v. *Swain et al.* and he crafted his opinion carefully and succinctly. He easily dismissed Slidell's first argument, that the agreement of one partner could not bind the other, by pointing out that the partnership had inhabited the building for two months. Citing section 2845 of the *Louisiana Code*, Martin opined that

26. It is ironic that Slidell took this approach, as he himself was an avid common lawyer and a staunch promoter of the reception of common law in Louisiana. In later years as a jurist, Slidell would set the standards for Louisiana's jurisprudence in the area of partnership law—the aspect of Louisiana's private law that completely eschews civil law in favor of common law remedies. See F. Hodge O'Neal, "An Appraisal of the Louisiana Law of Partnership," *Louisiana Law Review* 9 (1949): 326–7; cf. Fernandez, "From Chaos to Continuity," 30.

even if the Swains had negotiated the contracts without the authority of the other partners, they could be considered binding if the partnership had benefitted from the arrangement. As far as Martin was concerned, the fact that the firm occupied the premises for two months provided sufficient proof that Swain's partners had accepted and profited from the agreement.[27]

Slidell's second point, that Reynolds filed suit prematurely and that neither *Christy* v. *Casanave* nor the Roman law still applied after 1828, occupied the major portion of Martin's decision. In addressing this issue, Martin proceeded cautiously. He pointed out that the *Louisiana Code* and its accompanying repealing legislation indeed nullified the "Spanish, Roman, and French laws, which were in force in this state when Louisiana was ceded to the United States." Martin also cited section 3521 of the *Louisiana Code,* which noted that the acts of the legislative council, the former territorial legislature, and the present state assembly also had been repealed "in every case, which are specifically provided for by that code." But Martin went on to conclude that "the repeal spoken of in the code and the act of 1828, cannot extend beyond the laws which the legislature itself had enacted, that is, the laws in the 1825 *Louisiana Code;* for it is they alone which it may repeal." Martin concluded that the 1825 code and the repealing legislation invalidated only those older laws that it specifically addressed.

Furthermore, in regard to the influence of foreign laws on Louisiana's jurisprudence, Martin followed the interpretation of the great English commentator Sir William Blackstone in pointing out that only positive or written law informed "the civil or municipal law, that is, the rule by which particular districts, communities, or nations are governed"[28] and that they did not extend to

> those unwritten laws which do not derive their authority from the positive institution of any people, as the revealed law, the natural law, the law of nations, the laws of peace and war, and those laws

27. *Reynolds* v. *Swain et al.,* 193.
28. Blackstone, *Commentaries,* 1: 44.

which are founded in those relations of justice that existed in the nature of things, antecedent to any positive precept.

We, therefore, conclude, that the Spanish, Roman, and French civil laws, which the legislature repealed, are the positive, written or statute laws of those nations, and of this state; and only such as were introductory of a new rule, and not those which were merely declaratory—that the legislature did not intend to abrogate those principles of law which had been established or settled by the decisions of courts of justice.[29]

Martin argued that the repealing act voided only the positive, written laws that were in force in Louisiana prior to 1828. The 1828 act, however, did not repeal judicial decisions. The judge agreed that the decision in *Christy* v. *Casanave* was not grounded in Spanish or Louisiana statutes. Martin conceded that he knew of no Roman or French statute in force in Louisiana at the time of cession to which the repealing measure of either the code or the 1828 act could extend. Despite these facts, Martin went on to argue that "it is the daily practice in our courts to resort to the laws of Rome and France, and the commentaries on those laws, for the elucidation of principles applicable to analagous [*sic*] cases. Although the Roman law, on which the case of Christy v. Cazanave [*sic*] was determined, had no intrinsic authority here, the reason that dictated that law has great cogency."[30]

According to Martin, such cogency, in tandem with the daily practice in Louisiana to resort to foreign authorities, validated the district judge's remedy. Accordingly, Martin upheld the decision of the district court.

Slidell's second argument failed and Swain & Co. lost their appeal. But Slidell's contentions forced the Supreme Court of Louisiana to define its procedures in regard to foreign laws and the role of jurisprudence in Louisiana's judicial system. Speaking for the court, François Martin rejected the civilian approach to judicial proceedings in favor of the Anglo-American style of judicature. Law codes and legislative statutes made up an im-

29. *Reynolds* v. *Swain et al.,* 193.
30. Ibid.

portant part of Louisiana's legal heritage, but according to Martin the rights of independent judges to consult precedent and foreign authorities played an equally important role in the deliberations of Louisiana's judges. Martin affirmed the practices that had informed Louisiana's courts since the territorial period and put to rest the notion that Louisiana's high courts should function as civilian tribunals—as slaves to an inflexible series of codes.[31]

Martin's decision meant that Louisiana's supreme court could continue functioning in the manner it always had. In that regard, the judges of the Supreme Court of Louisiana worked in exactly the same fashion as their brethren on Virginia's Supreme Court of Appeals. Louisiana's supreme court could employ judicial decisions and consult foreign authorities just as any other American tribunal.

Reynolds v. *Swain et al.* ensured that the Anglo-American judicial style Louisiana had adopted in the territorial period would continue to define the role of the judiciary for the rest of the century. Civil law remained important to Louisiana's jurisprudence; indeed, civilian doctrines were becoming important to many American jurisdictions in the nineteenth century. The judicial style that *Reynolds* v. *Swain et al.* reaffirmed for Louisiana ensured that the state's judges could continue to consult and employ remedies other than the state's codes. In that regard foreign as well as common law precepts continued to invade Louisiana's legal discourse regularly after 1839.[32]

As important as Martin's decision in *Reynolds* v. *Swain et al.* was, however, the implications of the case evaded the understanding of most Louisianians in the mid–nineteenth century. If the supreme court received any notice at all, it came in the form of criticism about the long delays that resulted from backed-up dockets and in the cries for reform that punctu-

31. Ibid.
32. On the matter of common law precepts invading Louisiana's jurisprudence, the evidence is profound. The number of cases that were decided on the basis of English and American common law authorities is so prominent that it is impossible to display them here. Moreover, by midcentury entire areas of the law such as criminal law and partnership law had become thoroughly Americanized.

ated the drive for a new state constitutional convention in the 1840s. Critics, both in the nineteenth and twentieth centuries, have focused on the impotency of the Martin court as an expression of the difficulty related to the interpretation of civilian traditions in the state's legal system by a poorly trained judiciary and bar. Nothing could be further from the truth. Under both Mathews and Martin, Louisiana attracted a competent pool of jurists trained in both the Anglo-American and civilian traditions. Far from being well-intentioned boobs who mingled traditions arbitrarily to do the "best they could for their day," Louisiana's judges and lawyers moved easily within both systems and adopted measures from each that ensured the traditions most important to the state's residents and most applicable to the American tradition of justice. Indeed, the features of private law preserved in Louisiana became the model for similar code-sponsored legislation throughout the American South and West.

In all other matters and in terms of judicial behavior, Louisiana's legal system exhibited the same traditions and trends as other American jurisdictions. The role of the Supreme Court of Louisiana in dictating this style and policing its continuation by establishing precise rules of procedure, interpreting both the *Digest* and the 1825 code (especially in *Reynolds* v. *Swain et al.*) as foundations for *stare decisis,* and by setting the standards for the state's bar, played a fundamental role in this development.

The reforms of Livingston and his supporters barely altered the basic jurisdictional orientation of the state's judicial system. Martin and his brother judges saw to that.[33] In the successful battle against codification that culminated in *Reynolds* v. *Swain et al.,* the judges ensured that the "evils" of the common law system, as Livingston described them, would become a standard feature of nineteenth-century law in Louisiana. As Livingston predicted, this caused a measure of uncertainty and confusion. The problems that resulted from the judges' protection of the common law paled in comparison to the instability that permeated the bench in the 1830s and early 1840s when illness, political ambition, and the combustible nature of François-Xavier Martin combined to create a court in chaos.

33. For an analysis of those reforms, see Fernandez, "From Chaos to Continuity," 19–36.

6

FROM CHAOS TO CONTINUITY
Early Reforms

The problems of creating a common law and the judges' resistance to codification represented only part of the story of the supreme court's early years. Louisiana's 1812 constitution had created only the barest of outlines for the bench. While the legislators, judges, and jurisconsults argued about matters of law, the fuzzy definition of the court's makeup, its personnel, and its role in a rapidly changing society conspired to create a screwy system that by the mid-1830s cried out for reform. Significant revisions, however, required constitutional action. During the 1830s and 1840s the court faced serious challenges from an aggressive legislature, aging judges, and administrative malaise. Criticism of the supreme court mounted until the constitution of 1845 brought a measure of continuity to the chaotic situation.

One of the more vexing problems the court faced stemmed from the unsettled nature of its personnel. Louisiana's 1812 constitution had created lifetime judgeships and failed to institute a mechanism for effective judicial leadership. Over the course of the court's early history, the judges themselves adopted a system of judicial administration based on seniority, with the longest-tenured lawgiver serving as "senior" or "chief" judge. This system worked, for the most part; however, instability on the bench, coupled with "growing pains," led to several crises during the 1830s and 1840s.

The senior judges served with varying degrees of success. Dominick

Hall, the first senior judge, lasted only five months, resigning his seat for a federal appointment even before the court convened for the first time. His successor, George Mathews, was the first significant ranking judge, but during his tenure only a few cases hit the docket, so the judges settled the caseload expeditiously. Squabbles over the common law and codification then emerged as the dominant features of Mathews's term. When François-Xavier Martin assumed the role of senior judge, latent problems resulting from the court's imprecise definition began to surface.[1]

Population growth, the financial crisis of 1837, a rising number of appeals, an impractical circuit schedule, lack of a clearly prescribed system of rules of procedure, and the justices' declining health led to clogged dockets in the mid-1830s, when Martin became chief judge.[2] After George Mathews died in 1836, Judge Henry Adams Bullard resigned his seat to become Louisiana's new secretary of state.[3] To fill these vacancies and to help Martin combat the gargantuan caseload, the governor appointed George Eustis and Pierre Adolphe Rost to the bench. These young judges set out to reform the court's procedures in order to dispatch the greater number of cases, but Martin vigorously opposed their efforts. His steadfast resistance to the new judges' innovations forced both to resign within four months.[4] Moreover, Martin's insistence on remaining on the bench despite failing eyesight limited his ability to render decisions fast enough to reduce the burgeoning caseload.[5]

Public displeasure with the judiciary's handling of its own affairs compounded the court's internal problems. Gustavus Schmidt, a prominent New Orleans attorney and the court's most zealous critic at the time, observed that "the practice pursued by the Court, and the rules adopted by

1. Billings, *Historic Rules,* 85.

2. Gustavus Schmidt, "On the Administration of Justice in Louisiana," *Louisiana Law Journal* 1 (1842): 151.

3. Dora J. Bonquois, "The Career of Henry Adams Bullard, Louisiana Jurist, Legislator, and Educator," *Louisiana Historical Quarterly* 23 (1940): 1029.

4. Henry Plauché Dart, "The History of the Louisiana Supreme Court," *Louisiana Historical Quarterly* 4 (1921): 36.

5. Bonquois, "Career of Henry Adams Bullard," 1027.

it, are far from being convenient, or suited to the dispatch of business."[6] Furthermore, Schmidt chastised the judges for devoting only twelve to fifteen hours per week to hearing arguments and spending the rest of their time writing lengthy decisions. He labeled the tribunal a "talking Court"[7] because of the judges' irritating habit of interrupting counsel in the middle of arguments. Schmidt also voiced the dissatisfaction of the public and the bar over the justices' cavalier attitude toward holding regular hearings. He pointed out that at the height of the Panic of 1837, while appeals were mounting and the dockets were backing up, the judges let more than four months go by without a session.[8]

Meanwhile, as inept procedures and continuing personnel problems precipitated the court's gradual collapse, Democrats, seeking to recast the state's government into a more representative model of Jacksonian democracy, called for a new constitution.[9] The resulting constitutional convention provided a perfect device for Louisiana's statesmen to use to restructure the crumbling court. Delegates realized that the court's organization inadequately accommodated the state's growing needs for judicial appeal. Unlike their predecessors, who possessed only vague notions of what role the supreme court should assume in the state government, the new delegates could view the shortcomings of the past three decades as examples of areas in need of clarification and reform. Accordingly, the

6. Schmidt, "On the Administration of Justice," 156.

7. Schmidt did not coin the term "talking court." Henry Plauché Dart attributed the term to Schmidt in his centenary speech (reprinted in the article "The History of the Louisiana Supreme Court"), but this quote has been attributed to Schmidt in so many publications, such as the *Dictionary of American Biography,* that it requires clarification. To be sure, Schmidt's description of the court's procedures warrants such an interpretation.

8. Schmidt, "On the Administration of Justice," 157–8.

9. Joe Gray Taylor, *Louisiana: A Bicentennial History* (New York: W. W. Norton, 1976), 85. One significant aspect of the convention that Taylor raised was that the Democrats were quite shocked when the Whigs matched their representation in the convention. Ironically, many of the results of that convention may be viewed as reactions to Jacksonian corruption. For the most comprehensive analysis of the 1845 constitution, see Judith K. Schafer, "Reform or Experiment? The Constitution of 1845," in Billings and Haas, *In Search of Fundamental Law,* 21–36.

debates of the convention shed light on how the delegates sought to rectify the problems with the court's organization.

One of the more pressing problems the delegates tackled was the infirmity of the court's personnel. In the late 1830s, stopgap attempts to bolster the court's membership by adding judges had failed. As a consequence, the delegates sought new solutions. Following the examples of other states in the antebellum period, the delegates created the office of chief justice to handle all of the time-consuming administrative tasks. Moreover, the delegates recognized that one of the most serious obstacles to the development of a strong bench in the past had been that life tenure subjected the court to possible debilitating exactions of old age. As a remedy they shortened the justices' terms to eight years. Furthermore, they had the new judges draw lots to stagger the retirement order so that the entire court would not step down at the same time. And, to make the court more democratic, some of the Whig delegates proposed that supreme court justices should be elected. That motion, however, failed.[10] The question of electing supreme court justices as a measure to combat patronage on the court remained a hot issue until the next constitutional convention.[11]

Realizing that decent salaries would attract competent judges, the delegates then turned their attention to that crucial issue. Quite characteristically, the Jacksonian faction in the convention immediately proposed to set them at a staggering sum of $7,000, but the Whigs, led by former Democrat Isaac T. Preston, opposed this measure. Preston argued that such a figure would attract ambitious lawyers who wished to use the bench for their own profit. Preston carried his point and the convention lowered the salaries to $6,000 for the chief justice and $5,500 for the associate justices—still a tidy sum, but low enough to allay Preston's fears.[12]

10. *Journal of the Proceedings of the State of Louisiana, 1844–1845* (New Orleans, 1845), 195–7 [hereafter cited as JPSL].

11. Benjamin Wall Dart, *Constitutions of the State of Louisiana and Select Federal Laws* (Indianapolis: Bobbs-Merrill, 1932), 528. For the most extensive treatment of the Constitution of 1852, see Wayne M. Everard, "Louisiana's 'Whig' Constitution Revisited: The Constitution of 1852," in Billings and Haas, *In Search of Fundamental Law*, 37–51.

12. JPSL, 197–201.

Another aspect of the convention's judiciary article was the debated issue of reconciling the writ of habeas corpus with Louisiana's civil law traditions, which provided no model for tailoring such common law rights. The delegates, like their predecessors in 1812, were still unsure of whether supreme court justices should have the right to issue the writ, and how far their rights should have jurisdiction. After much debate the delegates decided to allow the justices to grant the writ in cases brought before the supreme bench.[13]

One important aspect of the debates revealed a conscious attempt by the delegates to relieve pressure on the dockets. Several members proposed a raise in the minimum monetary limit of cases eligible for review from three to five hundred dollars. Such a measure had been common in court reforms since the beginning of judicial institutions. In Louisiana's case this step would drastically reduce the number of cases before the bench; but in the mid-1840s three hundred dollars was still a handsome sum of money. The delegates decided not to change the limit.[14] Although this particular attempt at reform failed, it clearly illustrated the mood of the delegates. The men responsible for the reform of the court realized that its appellate powers must serve the greater interests of the state's citizens. Of course, they wanted the court to operate smoothly, but the desire for precision in the court's methods could not supersede the needs of the people.

Finally, the delegates focused on the inclusion of criminal appeals into the court's jurisdiction. Between 1843 and 1845 a court of errors and appeals handled criminal appeals, but the court did not work very well, and the prospect of having two separate courts to deal with these matters was not promising. Most supreme courts around the country heard criminal appeals, and it seemed possible that with a bit of restyling, the Louisiana supreme court could also. The movement to bring criminal law under the eye of the state supreme court indicates the continuing struggle of the state's leaders to fit common law practices into their civilian legal traditions. This contest exhibited itself in the manner in which the court dealt

13. Ibid., 189.
14. Ibid., 197, 225.

with its criminal jurisdiction. The practice of hearing appeals only when errors of interpretation or points of law existed consciously mirrored the practices of England's Court of King's Bench as set forth by Joseph Chitty.[15] Inclusion of criminal law into the jurisdiction of the state supreme court marked a major change.[16] Now a single court handled all criminal appeals. Such a measure tightened the appellate structure of the state's court system. Also, it gave the supreme court a whole new area of jurisdiction. Taking on that fresh authority would be no easy task for the court, but the addition of criminal appeals reflected the delegates' confidence in the ability of their constitutional reforms to trim the docket sufficiently to make the extra burden manageable.

The changes the convention adopted in 1845 reflected a conscious attempt at judicial reform. Delegates to that convention were dissatisfied with the operations of the previous court and the makeshift attempts used to correct them. In creating the office of chief justice, they exhibited an understanding of the procedures of other state courts around the country. By limiting the term of judicial appointments to eight years, observing caution in the discussion of judicial salaries, and (though unsuccessfully) calling for the election of justices, the delegates echoed a nationwide cry for reform that had developed by midcentury to combat the corruption of the Jacksonian spoils system. Moreover, the delegates displayed an interest in the ongoing struggle to align Louisiana's judicial practices with American jurisprudence by seeking to define the supreme court's powers of habeas corpus and by adding criminal appeals to the court's jurisdiction. These changes marked a deliberate attempt to cast Louisiana's judiciary into a more representative model of American jurisprudence. They also illustrated a connection between Louisiana's convention and the reform spirit of other state conventions in the middle of the nineteenth century.[17]

15. Albert Voorhies, *A Treatise on the Criminal Jurisprudence of Louisiana*, vol. 1 (New Orleans, 1860), 45. For a comprehensive analysis of the court of errors and appeals, see Sheridan E. Young, "Louisiana's Court of Errors and Appeals, 1843–1846," in Billings and Fernandez, *A Law unto Itself?* 99–116.

16. JPSL, 189.

17. Hurst, *Lawmakers*, 126–7. See also Taylor, *Bicentennial History*, 85.

As a result of that climate of change, the delegates created a new supreme court vastly different from its predecessor. The court also had gained an official chief justice who assumed responsibility for organizing and leading the court. The three new associate judges could look to the authority of the chief justice in hope of more efficient leadership in the handling of the demanding caseload. Replacing the lifetime appointments with eight-year term limits shielded the court from the problems of age and complacency, and staggering the terms ensured the continuation of experienced leadership. Although the constitution preserved the November-through-June New Orleans session, the justices could schedule their itinerary as need arose, rather than having to submit to a grueling, impractical travel regulation. Preston lost his bid for a modest increase in judicial salaries.[18]

As the convention met, the old court wound up its operations. Although the dockets remained bloated, the appointment in 1840 of Alonzo Morphy, Henry Adams Bullard, Edward Simon, and Rice Garland solved the problem of a depleted bench.[19] Martin worked more easily with these men than with Eustis and Rost. Rice Garland, however, inflicted a final wound on the Martin court's reputation when he became embroiled in a criminal scandal. Garland had come to the court with a spotless reputation. A leader in the Whig party with close ties to Henry Clay,[20] he also had drawn notice from the Democrats because of his coauthorship of the influential pamphlet *A Plan of the Standing Army of 200,000 Men.*[21] Thus, an allegation that Garland demeaned his office caught his brother justices and everyone else by surprise.

Garland's troubles began on October 22, 1845, when he sent his agent, Major J. A. Beard, to deliver a $6,000 promissory note to J. Kilty Smith. The note bore John McDonogh's signature, but Smith immediately ques-

18. Dart, *Constitutions of Louisiana,* 513.

19. Bonquois, "Career of Henry Adam Bullard," 1029.

20. Rice Garland to Henry Clay, October 11, 1831, Henry Clay Collection, *The Papers of Henry Clay,* DLC-HC, 34 vols, reel 4 (Library of Congress, Washington, D.C., 1925).

21. May 26, 1840, *The Papers of Martin Van Buren* (Library of Congress, Washington, D.C., 1911), vol. 39, reel 23.

tioned the note's authenticity because it was crumpled and soiled. Beard explained that the note was in poor condition because Garland had dropped it in the gutter. Smith took the note but remained skeptical. As fate would have it, McDonogh dropped by Smith's brokerage firm later that day on another errand. Smith showed McDonogh the note and asked if the signature was authentic. McDonogh conceded that the signature looked like his, but could not remember ever signing a note for that amount for the judge. On closer investigation, he saw that the signature was indeed his own, but that the note itself was forged. Evidently, the judge had lifted the words off of one of McDonogh's old letters by some chemical process and had written in the terms of the promissory note. McDonogh repudiated the document and counseled Smith to get his money from Garland as soon as possible.[22]

McDonogh's renunciation outraged Smith. He sent for Garland, but the judge refused to see him and sent his agent to apologize. Evidently, Smith's wrath frightened Garland, and the judge himself paid a visit to McDonogh the next day. At first McDonogh rebuffed Garland's urgent request to honor the note, but then the judge proceeded to make a spectacle of himself. First he threatened suicide, then he paraded his children before McDonogh and tearfully begged the man to save him. Garland's plea so moved McDonogh that he took up the note and even endorsed another for $2,800 to help Garland out of further difficulties.[23]

At this point the men could have resolved the whole matter quietly, but such a story could not remain secret in New Orleans for long. On 8 December 1845, Garland walked into the supreme court chamber in New Orleans and found Martin and the other judges discussing allegations that Garland had taken a bribe. Garland demanded a chance to defend himself, but Martin refused and abruptly adjourned the session. The *Daily Picayune* reported this confrontation the next day and the rumors became a news event. In light of the impending public scandal over the integrity of a brother justice, Martin and his colleagues decided to turn the matter over to the Second District Court for investigation.[24]

22. *New Orleans Bee*, December 11, 1845.
23. Ibid.
24. *New Orleans Daily Picayune*, December 9, 1845.

After McDonogh and Smith gave depositions to the parish court, Garland had to face the public ridicule he so desperately tried to avoid. Apparently it was too much for him, for on 10 December he tried to commit suicide by leaping from a steamboat docked near the levee, but the alert crew saved him from drowning. Undeterred, Garland broke free and tried to jump in again, but spectators stopped him before he could climb the railing. Judge Garland was then taken home in a state of exhaustion.[25]

Naturally, the press took a dim view of the whole affair. The *Picayune* reported "a more terrible retribution never yet overtook an offender against the laws of the land. Himself [Garland] a high priest of the law. He has fallen under its dreadful denunciation."[26] The *Bee* was a bit more sympathetic. However, it questioned the judge's mental health: "We deeply regret to have to state that the late reports prejudicial to the character and standing of Judge Garland, of the supreme bench, have had a melancholy effect upon his mind."[27] At this point, Garland could not face the wrathful public, and before the authorities filed charges, the distraught judge "fled to Texas."[28]

The Garland affair marked the final chapter of the history of the first Supreme Court of Louisiana. It was a sad, yet somehow fitting end to the troubled tribunal. Even as the scandal unfolded, the constitutional convention wound down its preparations to reorganize the state government. The Garland scandal focused public attention on the court as never before, and it pressured the new justices to move quickly to repair the court's tattered reputation. By the beginning of March 1846, George Eustis, the new chief justice of Louisiana, entered the courtroom in New Orleans. His colleagues Pierre Adolphe Rost, George Rogers King, and Thomas

25. The *Bee* and the *Picayune* offer slightly different versions of the episode, therefore it is not clear whether the steamboat in question was the *F. M. Streck* or the *Sultana*.

26. *New Orleans Daily Picayune*, December 11, 1845.

27. *New Orleans Bee*, December 12, 1845.

28. The term "fled to Texas" is fitting here because it was a term in the legal jargon of nineteenth-century Louisiana for persons who left the state to escape financial problems. Actually, the newspapers published many conflicting accounts of Garland's whereabouts in the early months of 1846. At one point, the judge was even believed to be dead; however, he did not die until the 1860s. Billings, *Historic Rules*, 85.

Slidell took their seats with him. As his first official act, Eustis read the commissions that proclaimed the appointments of the justices and the organization of the court. Then he recognized the bailiff, General John L. Louis, and instructed him to declare the court officially in session. The bailiff obeyed, and his announcement received a thundering round of applause from the lawyers and spectators in the chamber.[29] These new justices all possessed specific talents that helped the court begin its new era in the easiest possible fashion.

When the new justices took up their appointments, they accepted the challenge to transform the supreme court into a respectable and efficient body of appeal. Their paramount task was to correct the structural defects that had plagued the court since its beginning. Their talents enhanced their chances of success.

As the state's first chief justice, George Eustis was a natural. A prominent member of the New Orleans bar, Eustis had a long career in state politics. Emigrating from Boston, he served as state attorney general, secretary of state, a justice of the supreme court, and a delegate to the 1845 convention.[30] He led the Louisiana office of the Adams campaign in the 1824 presidential election and was involved in other unofficial capacities.[31] Having served under Martin, Eustis had experienced the problems of the old court and he understood the docket crisis, which he had endeavored to correct. He also brought to his tasks a firm grounding in Anglo-American legal precepts in addition to a good grasp of national politics.

Eustis's colleagues possessed equally valuable qualifications. Pierre Rost, a French immigrant, had served in the state legislature before his first appointment to the court in 1839.[32] Along with Eustis, with whom he shared similar views about reforming court procedures, Rost provided continuity on the post-1845 court. He also added the experience of a trained civilian who saw the need to harmonize civil law precepts with

29. *New Orleans Daily Picayune,* March 20, 1846.

30. Billings, *Historic Rules,* 90–1.

31. Joseph G. Tregle, Jr., *Louisiana in the Age of Jackson: A Clash of Cultures and Personalities* (Baton Rouge: Louisiana State University Press, 1999), 161, 178, 227.

32. Billings, *Historic Rules,* 90–1.

common law traditions. While still a young man, he retired from the court in 1853, and ended his political career as the Confederate commissioner to Spain.[33]

George Rogers King, like his brother justices, had been an active participant in Louisiana politics, but he also brought singular gifts to the court.[34] He was its first member to have practiced criminal law. A onetime district attorney, King had recently served as chief judge of the defunct court of errors and appeals.[35] As a consequence, he was one of but three judges in the entire state who had begun to wrestle with the question of how to adopt the concept of allowing felons the right to appeal their convictions to a higher judicial authority. He wrote all of the court of errors and appeals opinions. Those decisions rested on common law precedents, and so his influence on criminal law before and after 1846 was profound.[36]

Unlike his colleagues, Thomas Slidell had not held public office before coming to the court. Nevertheless, the name Slidell was well known throughout the state because of the reputation of his brother, John. But Thomas Slidell possessed a fine legal mind and was an expert on the laws of partnership.[37] As a justice, Slidell's most important contributions were in that field of law. Between 1846 and 1852 he wrote every decision in which the laws of partnership were at issue. His opinions displayed a fondness for common law principles and the use of these sources to define commercial relationships within the state's body of law. When taken together with other Anglo-American influences on the creation of the court

33. James W. Cortada, "Pierre Rost-Denis and Confederate Diplomacy: A Reevaluation," *Louisiana Historical Quarterly* 54 (1971), 18.

34. Billings, *Historic Rules*, 93.

35. Sidney Joseph Aucoin, "Political Career of Isaac Johnson, Governor of Louisiana, 1846–1850," *Louisiana Historical Quarterly* 28 (1945): 956–7. See, for example, Dart, "History of the Supreme Court," *Louisiana Historical Quarterly* 4 (1921): 39; Young, "Court of Errors and Appeals."

36. *Reports of Cases Argued and Determined in the Supreme Court of Louisiana* (St. Paul: West Publishing, 1910), vols. 1 to 3, passim; Young, "Court of Errors and Appeals."

37. O'Neal, "Louisiana Law of Partnership," 326–7; see, for example, William K. Dart, "The Justices of the Supreme Court," *Louisiana Historical Quarterly* 4 (1921), 118.

itself, as well as the impact of common law literature on the required reading for prospective lawyers, Slidell's role in bringing the court more in concert with a larger American legal tradition marked a significant reform.

Because he drew a short term, Judge King rotated off the court in 1850.[38] Governor Isaac Johnson appointed Isaac Trimble Preston to replace him.[39] Preston, a native of Virginia, had actively participated in Louisiana politics for a long time. He was an old adversary of Eustis, having been a Jackson supporter in the 1824 and 1828 elections. Preston profited from his support of Jackson and his close personal friendship. Customs collector Martin Gordon, one of Louisiana's most important Jacksonian power brokers, appointed Preston to several important posts after the 1828 election. Preston showed his integrity, however, when he refused to support the corrupt Gordon in a bid for the governorship in 1830.[40] Thereafter, Preston turned away from the state's Democrats and became a Whig, which in turn led to a close friendship with Henry Clay.[41] Preston was also a booster of New Orleans society. His wealth and vast real estate holdings led him to donate lands for the Methodist Episcopal church in Carrollton in 1843 while he resided in the suburb.[42] As attorney general he built a reputation for legal scholarship and personal integrity. Elected to the constitutional convention of 1845, he spearheaded the push for low judicial salaries,[43] and perhaps as a result of his association with Gordon, he tried to keep the new court free of patronage and nepotism. Despite this early promise, Preston's impact on the court was negligible because he died tragically in a steamboat accident on Lake Pontchartrain in July 1852.[44]

38. H. P. Dart, *Constitutions of Louisiana*, 513–4.

39. Billings, *Historic Rules*, 99.

40. Tregle, *Louisiana in the Age of Jackson*, 205–20, 256–60, 366–422.

41. Padgett, "Letters of James Brown," 1152.

42. William H. Williams, "The History of Carrollton," *Louisiana Historical Quarterly* 22 (1939): 209, 213.

43. JPSL, 197–201. See also John T. Hood, "The Louisiana Judiciary," *Louisiana Law Review* 14 (1954): 811–24.

44. W. K. Dart, "Justices," 118.

William Dunbar replaced Preston. Dunbar's previous political experience was limited. In 1849 he and fellow Democrat W. W. Wood lost bids to the state senate when they opposed Whig candidates Judah P. Benjamin and James Robb. However, Dunbar remained friendly with his Whig opponents. This association eventually won him the seat on the high court. But Dunbar had relatively little impact on the court. Less than a year after his appointment, a new constitution reconstituted the bench.[45]

Each of these men demonstrated singular talents as judges. Eustis and Rost lent experience, reform ideas, and prior appellate service to the bench. Slidell brought his respectable name and talent in partnership law. Isaac Preston gave the court the use of his legal scholarship and undeniable dignity. And William Dunbar, with his bipartisan relationships, bolstered the court after the loss of Preston. The Garland affair turned the public eye toward the court, and the press marked every action of the new judges. As a consequence, their first activities as leaders of the state's judiciary concentrated on improving the efficiency of the bench.

One of the earliest tasks the new justices attempted was the correction of the court's rules of procedure. Before 1846 the court had used its rule-making powers sparingly and only as the need arose. Its rules were consequently scattered among thirty-two years of documentation. Judges, lawyers, and clerks of court faced a tedious and time-consuming challenge whenever they wished to research a rule or clarify a procedural impediment. To remedy this situation, the court immediately set out to compile the existing rules. The justices appointed a drafting committee in the spring of 1846. That committee presented its preliminary draft the following November, and, after making a few corrections of its own, the court promulgated a slightly revised version on December 7.[46]

To help expedite business, the new rules called for the creation of a "delay" docket. These regulations transferred all cases that stood on the general docket for eighteen months or more to the delay docket, where they remained until a break in the court's regular business permitted their

45. Harry Howard Evans, "James Robb, Banker and Pioneer Railroad Builder of Ante Bellum Louisiana," *Louisiana Historical Quarterly* 23 (1940): 202–4.

46. Billings, *Historic Rules*, 11–2.

hearing.[47] The rules also established special days and summary dockets to decide routine cases.[48] This measure ended all arguments over the court's right to issue writs of mandamus, prohibition, quo warranto, and certiorari and allowed the judges to dispatch cases from the summary docket at set intervals. The regular hearing of cases would no longer be impeded by arguments over the court's right to issue ordinary writs.

Moreover, the judges revamped some of the old rules to address new demands on the state's legal system. The revision of the rules governing requirements for candidates to the state bar represented the best example of the judges' new efficiency. First, to keep the task of examining prospective attorneys to a minimum, examinations were required at specified intervals.[49] Before 1846 an applicant could apply for his examination at any time, no matter how inconvenient the interruption would be to the court's business. Next, the judges added new writings, representing recent scholarship in American jurisprudence, into the reading list. The most conspicuous of these were Joseph Story's *Commentaries on the Constitution of the United States* and James Kent's *Commentaries on American Law*.[50] These additions to the syllabus reflected not only the judges' growing concern with the quality of legal education but also the resolve to provide young Louisiana lawyers with a firm grasp of American legal principles.

Restyling the court's rules signaled a major reform of procedure. The new judges provided the court with a single publication that future judges, clerks, and litigants before the supreme bench could use as a guide for the preparation of their cases. Eleven concise rules now distilled three decades' worth of regulations, which formerly were scattered through long and disorganized minute books and in published reports. Lawyers and judges could now consult a single reference work to clear up questions regarding the court's procedures. Moreover, this sweeping revision clarified the court's methods and helped to alleviate the pressure on the

47. Ibid., 42.
48. Ibid., 42–3.
49. Ibid., 45–6.
50. Ibid., 46–7.

dockets. The creation of the delay docket, the summary docket, and the assignment of special days for bar admissions solved crucial problems in the court's schedule and freed the justices from the time-consuming inconvenience of having to jostle the court's schedule to provide for certification of lawyers, settling long-docketed cases, and summary judgments. This measure restricted the regular docket to cases that warranted the court's immediate attention. Adding two important works on American law to the student's reading list also deserves notice because it illustrates the concern of the court's new judges with educating the state's new attorneys in the American judicial tradition.

But the revision of the court's rules marks only the beginning of the first reform of the supreme court. The court now had to illustrate, through its decisions, what role the reforms would play in the shaping of the state's jurisprudence. Accordingly, the success of these changes can be gauged only through performance. The improvements streamlined the court's ability to handle litigation and greatly facilitated its operations.

The constitutional revision and rule changes greatly increased the court's ability to settle litigation. Between 1813 and 1845 the supreme court decided 5,873 cases,[51] for an average of only 178 cases per year.[52] Under the revisions between 1846 and 1852, the court dispatched 2,903 cases[53] at an average of 414 cases per year.[54] Furthermore, in the previous period the largest number of cases decided in one year was 403, in 1841 when the supreme court had an unprecedented five justices. In 1844, the year immediately preceding the constitutional revision, the court decided

51. A chart of the number of cases per year from 1813 to 1845 is available in the files of Marie Windell at the University of New Orleans, Archives and Special Collections. Table 1 of this study is derived from that chart. These totals include only cases from the eastern district, since few records from the western district exist.

52. See Table 1.

53. This total omits cases handled by the first court in the transition period in 1846 and those handled by the second court in the transition period in 1853. See Table 1.

54. Henry Plauché Dart estimated the number of cases between 1813 and 1845 as forty to ninety per year, and between 1845 and 1852 as five to six hundred per year. However, these estimates cannot be verified by the record.

only 288 cases.[55] By early 1847 the new judges had cleared the docket (see Table 1).[56]

Straightening out the court's procedures was a major accomplishment, but the justices who sat on the court between 1846 and 1853 faced another, more difficult, task. They had to put the Garland scandal behind them. Moreover, they had to take charge of the constitutional revision of 1845 and make it work. The manner in which the court increased its ability to handle cases and the success of the court under its first chief justice illustrated the progress gained through the legislative revision. Reordering of

TABLE I

CASES TRIED PER YEAR IN THE LOUISIANA SUPREME COURT
IN THE EASTERN DISTRICT

Year	Cases	Year	Cases	Year	Cases
1813	27	1827	171	1841	403
1814	62	1828	161	1842	353
1815	41	1829	165	1843	361
1816	64	1830	186	1844	288
1817	67	1831	193	1845	300
1818	58	1832	187	1846*	291
1819	96	1833	118	1847	428
1820	114	1834	155	1848	429
1821	128	1835	168	1849	406
1822	107	1836	183	1850	414
1823	160	1837	206	1851	459
1824	154	1838	268	1852	476
1825	162	1839	267		
1826	119	1840	381		

Note: Statistics from the western district no longer exist.
*The 1846 total includes only cases tried by the new court.

55. See Table 1.

56. Supreme Court of Louisiana Docket Book, No. 5, June 29, 1843–January 13, 1845, Department of Archives and Manuscripts, Earl K. Long Library, University of New Orleans.

the court's rules and the procedures they defined proved to be the new justices' most effective endeavor.

Moreover, the actions of the men who sat on the bench exhibited integrity, diligence, and commitment. They faced a difficult and unprecedented task in reforming the court and they responded admirably. The court was not yet perfected. Future constitutional conventions and future antebellum justices continued to change the court as the judicial needs of the state evolved. The upheaval of the 1860s and 1870s further interrupted the workings of the court. But the reforms set out in 1845 marked the first major step forward in the evolution of the supreme court.

The history of the court from 1813 to 1852 reveals the manner in which Louisianians blended their legal practices into a representative model of American justice. For many years scholars have described the state's legal history as a clash of legal traditions. But the development of the supreme court illustrated a deliberate effort to harmonize the state's legal traditions with those of other states. Indeed, historians have placed too much emphasis on differences between Louisiana's legal system and others in the nation, and have ignored the important struggle of the state fathers to reconcile their legal institutions with American patterns of jurisprudence.

The supreme court's development evidenced that reconciliation. Drafters of Louisiana's early constitutions had no real idea of how to create a supreme court. Louisiana's Democrats called the 1845 convention with the sole intention of making the state into a more precise model of Jacksonian democracy. Whig victories in the campaign for delegates, however, reflected a nationwide spirit of reform born out of dissatisfaction with Jacksonian corruption.[57] The salary debate in the convention illustrated the collision of these two national trends.

Interpretation of the struggle to blend the two traditions required context. The philosophy underlying both the common law tradition and the civilian tradition, when viewed at the most basic level, is quite similar. America's premier legal historian, James Willard Hurst, echoing the thoughts of John C. Calhoun, argued that the role of law in any society

57. Taylor, *Bicentennial History*, 85.

is to protect the individual from society and vice versa.[58] Legal historians have overemphasized the subtle distinctions between the civil and common law traditions and their influences on the development of law in Louisiana.

From its inception Louisiana has struggled to pattern its judicial practices after those of other American states. No clash between the two legal traditions in Louisiana, though the concept has long been accepted, impeded the process. Louisiana lawyers and politicians did not fight alien American legal principles, rather they strove to reconcile the two into a working judicial order. Problems that plagued early incarnations of the court had little to do with the differences between the common law and civilian traditions. Problematic procedures, increased demands on the court, financial crisis in the 1830s, sickness, old age, and poor leadership created the backlog in the dockets that spawned public criticism. The Rice Garland affair merely focused public attention on the court at a crucial period in its history.

The first revision of the court revealed a great deal of the character of the state fathers and the men they chose to man the court. In the constitutional convention the delegates sought to correct both the personnel and structural problems that plagued the court, such as the terms of the justices, their travel schedule, and the lack of an official leader. Also, some delegates to the convention, such as Isaac Preston, sought to clear up any possible situations that would lead corrupt men to pursue the bench. Furthermore, the new justices who assumed the bench in 1846 took further measures to correct the court's structural problems. Reordering the court's rules was their most important accomplishment. But the new judges' impeccable credentials, integrity, and capacity for work impressed Louisianians. In many respects, their success, by example, superseded the structural revisions they sought to implement. The new judges gave the court an air of integrity and confidence at a time when those commodities seemed conspicuously absent. They proved their integrity and won the confidence of the people—essential ingredients to the success of any judicial institution.

58. Hurst, *Lawmakers,* 440.

Revision of the supreme court did not end in 1852. Subsequent constitutional conventions brought such innovations as elections of justices.[59] Only the federal occupation in 1862 put a stop to this process. Therefore, the revision of the supreme court in 1845 accomplished much more than relief of the state's appellate problems. Indeed, that revision illustrated a wider concern of the state's politicians and their constituency with the growing conception of Louisiana's place in the American milieu.

59. Dart, *Constitutions of Louisiana,* 528.

Epilogue

I n its early incarnations the Supreme Court of Louisiana borrowed much from civilian and common law jurisdictions; however, the judicial operations of the bench clearly favored Anglo-American traditions. By the time of the Civil War the court had finally settled on its character, its practices, and its procedures. From colony to territory, from chaos to continuity, the court emerged as a truly representative model of American justice. But the war wrought chaos of a different kind.

As the court emerged from the Civil War and Reconstruction, it faced a new judicial revolution. Again, it mirrored the experience of other American states. By the early twentieth century, the state's lawyers began to lament the lack of a civilian tradition in Louisiana. However, such a tradition had no roots in the court's history. The twentieth-century "civilian renaissance" that sprung from these ill-formed criticisms transformed the court, but ignored its historical origins.

Appendix

Civil Law and Common Law

A central point of this book is that Louisiana under American rule, because of the background of its judges and lawyers, developed an important common law tradition to accompany its civilian heritage in the creation of a mixed jurisdiction and is not so alien to the American system of justice as has been previously suggested. To understand the implications of the interaction between civil law and common law in such a mixed jurisdiction, it is necessary to define each term, and to discuss what the intermingling of the two systems means in regard to legal change and development.

Civil law has two precise definitions. The first distinguishes the "municipal law" of a given community, that is, its "civil or private rights and remedies as contrasted with criminal laws" which derive from the "laws of nature" or "international law."[1] This definition applies to all modern jurisdictions, and is not a concern of this study. The second definition of civil law refers to a system of law pioneered by the Romans. Written codes represent the most important authorities of the civil law; however, judicial decisions sometimes play a minor role in resolving civil law disputes. Civil law judges are rigidly restricted to applying appropriate code citations to arrive at their decisions. Accordingly, the duties of the civil law judge leave little room for judicial interpretation of precedent, and the concept of judge-made law is alien to the system. After the fall of the Roman empire, civil law remained a popular tool for conflict resolution in Europe and became the backbone of the legal systems of many European

1. *Black's Law Dictionary,* s.v. "Civil Law."

countries, including France and Spain.[2] Since both France and Spain once controlled colonial Louisiana, the colony had developed a strong civilian heritage by the time Thomas Jefferson purchased it for the United States in 1803. Common law found its most profound expression in England and its colonies.

The common law is comprised of an infinite number of principles and social rules that have developed from time-honored customs and usages, judicial decisions that are based on those customs, all statutory and case law made in England and pre-Revolutionary America, and the positive law and juristic theory of any country of a general and universal nature.[3] In common law jurisdictions, emphasis on custom and usage and judicial decisions distinguishes judges from their civilian brethren because the ability to interpret those decisions and customs allows them greater flexibility. Moreover, once a common law judge renders a decision, his or her judgment becomes a part of the common law as well. Rather than functioning as a mere technician, the common law judge actually "makes law" every time he or she decides a case.

Since civil law and common law developed in different regions under varied circumstances, they occasionally differ greatly over certain substantive issues. For instance, in regard to the laws of descents the English showed a strong preference for the convention of primogeniture. Under civil law, descents were settled by a policy of "forced heirship," which simply meant that an heir's rights to share the inheritance were guaranteed under the law. Another distinction may be seen in the realm of criminal law. In common law jurisdictions, municipal statutes as well as an infinite variety of customs, usages, theories, and precedent all figure into a judge's decision. In civil law jurisdictions, municipal regulations alone offer remedies to the judge. Moreover, in common law the accused in a criminal case is presumed innocent and the burden to prove guilt falls on the state. Criminal defendants in civilian jurisdictions are considered guilty and must prove their innocence beyond a shadow of a doubt.

Louisiana represents neither a purely common law nor purely civil law

2. Ibid.
3. Ibid., "Common Law."

jurisdiction.[4] Louisiana adopted the common law, both the Anglo-American and the theoretical versions, as well as French and Spanish civil laws, at an early period in its judicial development under American rule. This may be seen in the procedural discussion of the Superior Court for the Territory of Orleans in chapter 3.

To what extent did common law inform the discourse of Louisiana's legal system? The answer is quite simple: common law traditions entered Louisiana's judicial discourse in three ways—through legislation, court rules, and judicial decisions.

The legislation that regulated judicial procedure and empowered the court to make its own rules in the territorial period continued in effect in Louisiana after it entered the Union. Subsequently, the writs that were established under these auspices bore the prescription that they be employed "according to the common law." Moreover, both the *Digest of 1808* and the 1825 Civil Code contained sections gleaned from the work of English authorities such as Sir Edward Coke's *Institutes* and Sir William Blackstone's *Commentaries*. Finally, Kerr's *Exposition of the Criminal Laws* originated in the works of English commentators, particularly Blackstone and Sir Matthew Hale. Thus, the common law entered Louisiana via legislation and the redaction of the state's various digests, expositions, and codes.[5]

4. One further distinction must be made here—"English law" does not necessarily mean "common law." Although common law in the form of statutes and judicial decisions formed the foundation of the British legal system, other kinds of law, for instance equity, as seen in the Court of Chancery, combined with the common law to constitute the British judicial system. Thus, when the term "common law" is used to describe English or American judicial practices, it is in a general and imprecise fashion, referring to a general acceptance of precedent in the absence of statutes as a basis for legal decisions, and to the binding nature of those decisions. Judicial decisions are not nearly as binding in civil law jurisdictions, where judges act merely as technicians in applying code citations and where judicial decisions are only rarely invoked to resolve disputes.

5. "An Act Regulating the Practice of the Superior Court in Civil Causes," *Orleans Acts,* 10 April 1805. A brief historiographical explanation must be considered here in regard to the contribution of Louisiana's redactors. The main redactor of both the *Digest* and the 1825 Civil Code was Louis Moreau Lislet, a French resident of New Orleans and one of the period's most prominent attorneys. Contemporary legal scholarship in Louisiana regards the

Court rules likewise allowed for common law reception as judges regulated their tribunal's proceedings under the guidelines laid out in enabling legislation. Attending to the various forms of writs and summonses issued by the judges was by far the most common way in which court rules allowed for common law reception. Jury trials, provided for in the

---

1808 *Digest* as the sole contribution of Moreau Lislet, offering no credit to Lislet's fellow jurisconsult, James Brown. Thus, Louisiana's legal scholars often react with surprise when citations from English commentators (Blackstone is by far the most common) are noted in studies of Louisiana's civil law. To understand why these references should not be surprising, it is necessary to probe the origins of the historiographical tradition that excludes common law as an element in Louisiana's legal settlement. These origins may be traced to a single source—see Batiza, "Origins of Modern Codification," 583. In the midst of a vigorous historiographical debate with Robert A. Pascal over the origins of Louisiana's civil code, Batiza was seeking to uncover the French sources of Louisiana's early codes. For the most part, Batiza's essay depends on a masterfully executed comparison of the *Digest* with various French and Spanish sources. As evidence for the importance of French sources, Batiza sought to emphasize Moreau Lislet's influence on the development of the *Digest.* Here Batiza argued that James Brown had nothing to do with the drafting of the *Digest,* basing his argument on an 1823 report to the Louisiana legislature that was designed to engineer a new compilation of the state's law. In the report Moreau Lislet stated that he alone drafted the 1808 *Digest.* But this evidence is flimsy, and at best, specious. In the first place, Moreau Lislet never protested the inclusion of James Brown's name on the published *Digest.* Certainly, if Moreau Lislet had done all of the work on the compilation, he would have complained to the legislature when Brown received half of the credit. Second, Moreau Lislet's statement is not substantiated in any way. Moreover, James Brown was never given an opportunity to respond to the claim. Finally, there is enough evidence to suggest that Moreau Lislet's claim may have been politically motivated. In the early 1820s, Louisiana, like many American states, was swept by a codification movement. Not only was the 1808 *Digest* inadequate for the state's legal needs, but it also lacked the authority of an official code. As preparations to draft a new code began in the legislature, partisan political divisions cropped up, as they did over any piece of legislation. When the legislature assigned a committee to study the possibilities of preparing a new code, a group of legislators identified with the "Creole faction" of the legislature seized control of the committee. In the first place, this cabal was not solely comprised of members of Louisiana's *ancienne population.* In fact, the leading figure of the interest group was Edward Livingston, an aggressive New York lawyer and entrepreneur. Livingston had long utilized the problem of integrating civil law and common law in Louisiana to his personal advantage. In the territorial period Livingston led the forces in favor of civilian reception and the drive for statehood. In both cases, he did so to oppose the forces loyal to Governor Claiborne, a group that often opposed Livingston's aggressive entrepre-

Practice Act of 1805, also forced the judges to devise their rules within the limits of common law practice. Finally, the responsibility of regulating a bar that relied on such common law devices allowed for further reception. As a matter of juristic theory, common law application in Louisiana has a more complicated background. To understand the implications of judicial contributions, it is first necessary to distinguish between the role of judges in civilian courts and in common law courts.

In the British and American traditions of common law, judges review litigants' petitions, hear viva voce examinations of witnesses, and, when appropriate, consider the recommendations of a jury in rendering their decisions. Often in deciding cases or pronouncing sentences, common law judges employ codified maxims and statute law. Since the common law is only partially codified, judges often are forced to look elsewhere for solutions to the cases before their benches. Sometimes a case will be settled on the basis of a single decision rendered in a previous trial. When a case is decided as such, it is considered settled by the principle of *stare decisis,* one of the cornerstones of English and American judicial theory. Accordingly, in common law jurisdictions the reputation of a court rests on the judge's ability to master mountains of jurisprudence. To achieve such mastery, judges are expected to hone their legal research skills and scholarship during lengthy apprenticeships as practicing attorneys. Theoretically, only the best lawyers are offered opportunities to ascend to the revered position of judge.[6]

In civilian jurisdictions, however, judges operate chiefly as judicial ad-

---

neurial schemes. A political outsider, Livingston tied his fortune to the so-called civilian faction of the legislature to ensure a measure of political prominence. For the most part he succeeded. As his junto postured to control the codification bill, Livingston managed to get himself appointed to the committee along with Moreau Lislet and another prominent Frenchman, Pierre Derbigny. Accordingly, the unsubstantiated statement in the committee's report must be taken with a grain of salt. Also, the utilization of common law authorities in the early codes also must be viewed in terms of the historical evidence. Even if Moreau Lislet's claim were true, he was a prominent member of the legal community and a frequent litigator before the supreme bench. Accordingly, Moreau Lislet, through years of practice, had become quite familiar with Anglo-American legal conventions. Why would he not use them when redacting the codes?

6. Baudouin, "Impact of the Common Law," 15–22.

ministrators. For the most part, judges are presented with written petitions from each litigant—the plaintiff makes his complaint and the defendant answers it. The judge then searches the various codes that make up the jurisdiction's laws in force and applies appropriate citations to render his or her decision. In the rare instances when the codes fail to present clear solutions, judges then turn to previous judicial decisions to inform their judgments. Unlike common law judges, civilian magistrates must uncover a long strain of consistent decisions in order to use them as the basis of a judgment. This procedure, known as *jurisprudence constante*, represents a lengthy and exhaustive process, and is rarely used in civilian courts. Moreover, *jurisprudence constante*, by requiring an immense string of consistent decisions, de-emphasizes the importance of individual decisions. And since no single decision of any civilian judge may be used to decide a case, the individual judge is far less powerful and creative in civil law jurisdictions than in common law jurisdictions. Because the method of rendering judgment in civilian systems requires such strict documentation and skills largely unnecessary to the advocate's practice of constructing and refuting complaints, prospective judges train for their positions in law school and assume the bench shortly after graduation. Thus, judges in civilian jurisdictions assume the role of trained technicians in a tightly restricted legal environment.[7]

The contrast between *stare decisis* (regarded widely as "judge-made law") in common law jurisdictions and the rarely used civilian doctrine of *jurisprudence constante* marks the salient difference between the role of the judge in civilian and common law jurisdictions. Common law judges are viewed as trusted lawgivers, seasoned by years of hard study and practical experience, and invested with power to interpret and to create crucial portions of their society's legal discourse. Civilian judges, as specialized technocrats, lack the creative power of common law magistrates and play less spectacular roles in their legal systems.

Pierre Clément de Laussat's suspension of the cabildo, which cast doubt on Louisiana's laws in force; the lack of a comprehensive code; and the Practice Act of 1805's provisions for jury trials, common law writs,

7. Ibid., 15–22.

and viva voce examinations forced Louisiana's judges to embrace the common law style of judicature. Moreover, the fact that from the territorial period to the federal occupation of Louisiana in 1862 the overwhelming majority of Louisiana's most powerful magistrates—its appellate judges—were Americans[8] (most possessing American legal educations) ensured the perpetuation of the judicial style of common law jurisdiction.

8. Billings, *Historic Rules,* Appendix 1, 43–50.

Selected Bibliography

For some court records both the published reports of the Supreme Court of Louisiana and the manuscript record are cited. For clarity's sake, manuscript records are cited only when they provide information not available in the published source.

Primary Sources

Acts Passed at the . . . of the Legislature of the State of Louisiana. New Orleans and Donaldsonville: 1813–1840.

Acts Passed at the . . . Legislative Council of the Territory of Orleans. New Orleans: 1804–1805.

Acts Passed at the . . . Legislature of the Territory of Orleans. New Orleans: 1807–1812.

Bayley, Sir John. *Summary of the Laws of Bills of Exchange, Cash Bills, and Promissory Notes.* London: E. Brooke, 1789.

Bergh, Albert Ellery, ed. *The Writings of Thomas Jefferson.* Washington, D.C.: Thomas Jefferson Memorial Foundation of the United States, 1903.

Billings, Warren M., ed. *The Historic Rules of the Supreme Court of Louisiana, 1813–1879.* Lafayette: Center for Louisiana Studies, University of Southwestern Louisiana, 1985.

Black, Henry Campbell. *Black's Law Dictionary: Definitions of the Terms and Phrases of American and English Jurisprudence, Ancient and Modern.* 5th ed. St. Paul: West Publishing, 1979.

Blackstone, Sir William. *Commentaries on the Laws of England.* 4 vols. Oxford: Clarendon Press, 1766–1769.

Bullard, Henry Adams. "A Discourse on the Life and Character of the Honorable François-Xavier Martin, Late Senior Judge of the Supreme Court." In *An Un-*

common Experience: Law and Judicial Institutions in Louisiana, 1803–2003, edited by Warren M. Billings and Judith Kelleher Schafer. Lafayette: Center for Louisiana Studies, University of Southwestern Louisiana, 1997.

Cabell Family Papers. Virginia Historical Society.

Calhoun, John C. "Disquisition on Government." In *Works of John C. Calhoun*. 6 vols. New York: D. Appleton, 1857–1864.

Call, Daniel. *Reports of Cases Argued and Adjudged in the Court of Appeals in Virginia*. Richmond: 1801–1833.

Carter, Clarence E., comp. *The Territorial Papers of the United States*. Vol. 9. Washington, D.C.: United States Government Printing Office, 1940.

Chitty, Joseph. *A Practical Treatise on Bills of Exchange, Checks on Banks, Promissory Notes, Bankers Cash Notes, and Bank Notes*. 1st American ed. Philadelphia: William P. Farranc, 1809.

Civil Code of the State of Louisiana. New Orleans: 1825.

Henry Clay Papers. Library of Congress.

Cooper, Thomas, trans. *The Institutes of Justinian*. Philadelphia: 1812.

Court of Pleas for the Territory of Orleans. *Minute Book*. City Archives, New Orleans Public Library, Louisiana Division.

Dart, Henry Plauché. "The History of the Supreme Court of Louisiana." Speech at the Centenary of the Louisiana Supreme Court. *Louisiana Annual Reports*. St. Paul: West Publishing, 1914.

De Laussat, Pierre Clément. *Memoirs of My Life*. Translated by Sister Agnes Josephine Pastwa, edited by Robert D. Bush. Baton Rouge: Louisiana State University Press, 1978.

Domat, Jean. *The Civil Laws in the Natural Order.* . . . Translated by William Strahan. London: J. Betterman for E. Bell, 1722.

Hening, William Waller, and William Munford. *Reports of Cases Argued and Determined in the Supreme Court of Appeals of Virginia*. 4 vols. Philadelphia: 1808–1811.

Hobson, Charles F. et al., eds. *The Papers of John Marshall*. Vol. 5. Chapel Hill: University of North Carolina Press in Association with the Institute of Early American History and Culture, 1987.

Journal of the Proceedings of the State of Louisiana, 1844–1845. New Orleans: 1845.

Kent, James. *Commentaries on American Law*. New York: O. Halsted, 1826.

Kerr, Lewis. *An Exposition of the Criminal Laws of the Territory of Orleans*. 1805. Reprint, New Orleans: Wm. W. Gaunt & Sons, 1986.

Leigh, Benjamin Watkins. *Reports of Cases Argued and Determined in the Court of Appeals, and in the General Court of Virginia*. Richmond: 1830–1831.

Edward Livingston Papers. Firestone Library, Princeton University.

Manuscript Records of the Superior Court for the Territory of Orleans. City Archives, New Orleans Public Library, Louisiana Division.

Martin, François-Xavier. *The History of Louisiana from the Earliest Period.* 2 vols. New Orleans: Lyman and Beardslee, 1827–1829.

——. *Reports of Cases Argued and Determined in the Supreme Court of Louisiana, 1809–1830.* 10 vols. New Orleans: 1846–1853.

New Orleans Bee, 1845–1853.

New Orleans Daily Picayune, 1845–1853.

"Ordinance of the Superior Council Regulating the Practice of Medicine, Surgery, and Obstetrics." In "The Cabildo Archives." *Louisiana Historical Quarterly* 3 (January–October, 1920): 86–9.

Padgett, James A., ed. "Letters of James Brown to Henry Clay, 1804–1835." *Louisiana Historical Quarterly* 24 (October 1941): 921–1177.

Phillipps, Samuel March. *A Treatise of the Law of Evidence.* New York: Gould, Banks, and Gould, 1816.

Pothier, Robert Joseph. *A Treatise on Obligations Considered in a Moral and Legal View.* London: J. Butterworth, 1806.

——. *A Treatise on Obligations Considered from a Moral and Legal View.* New Bern, N.C.: Martin and Ogden, 1802.

Randolph, Peyton. *Reports of Cases Argued and Determined in the Court of Appeals of Virginia.* 6 vols. Richmond: 1823–1830.

Robinson Family Papers. Virginia Historical Society.

Conway Robinson Papers. Virginia Historical Society.

Robinson, Merrit M. *Reports of Cases Argued and Determined in the Supreme Court of Louisiana.* New Orleans: Thomas Rea, 1847.

Rowland, Dunbar S. *The Official Letterbooks of W. C. C. Claiborne, 1801–1806.* 6 vols. Jackson, Miss.: State Department of Archives and History, 1917.

Russell, William Oldnall. *A Treatise on Crimes and Misdemeanors.* London: J. Butterworth, 1819.

Schmidt, Gustavus. "On the Administration of Justice in Louisiana." *Louisiana Law Journal* 1 (April 1842): 132–61.

Starkie, Thomas. *A Practical Treatise on the Law of Evidence and Digest in Proofs in Civil and Criminal Proceedings.* Philadelphia: P. H. Nicklin & T. Johnson, 1832.

Story, Joseph. *Commentaries on the Constitution of the United States.* Cambridge, Mass.: Brown Shattuck, 1833.

Supreme Court of Louisiana. Docket Books. Supreme Court of Louisiana Collection, Department of Archives and Special Collections, Earl K. Long Library, University of New Orleans.

Supreme Court of Louisiana Collection. Department of Archives and Special Collections, Earl K. Long Library, University of New Orleans.

Creed Taylor Papers. Special Collections, Alderman Library, University of Virginia.

Thorpe, Francis Newton, ed. *The Federal and State Constitutions, Colonial Charters and Organic Laws of the States, Territories, and Colonies, Now or Heretofore Forming the United States of America.* Vol. 1. Washington, D.C.: United States Government Printing Office, 1909.

United States Congress. *The Statutes at Large of the United States of America.* Compiled by Richard Peters. Boston: Little and Brown, 1845.

Upton, Wheelock S. *The Code of Practice in Civil Cases for the State of Louisiana.* New Orleans: E. Johns, 1838.

Martin Van Buren Papers. Library of Congress.

Vattel, Emmerich de. *The Law of Nations, or Principles of the Law of Nature, Applied to the Conduct and Affairs of Nations and Sovereigns.* London: G. G. J. and J. Robinson, etc., 1793.

Voorhees, Albert. *A Treatise on the Criminal Jurisprudence of Louisiana.* 2 vols. New Orleans: Bloomfield and Steel, 1860.

Washington, Bushrod. *Reports of Cases Argued and Determined in the Supreme Court of Appeals in Virginia.* 2 vols. Richmond: 1798–1799.

Secondary Sources

Aucoin, Sidney Joseph. "Political Career of Isaac Johnson, Governor of Louisiana, 1846–1850." *Louisiana Historical Quarterly* 28 (July 1945): 941–90.

Batiza, Rudolfo. "Origins of Modern Codification." *Tulane Law Review* 56 (February 1982): 477–601.

———. "The Louisiana Code of 1808: Its Actual Sources and Present Relevance." *Tulane Law Review* 46 (1972): 4–164.

———. "Sources of the Civil Code of 1808, Facts and Speculation: A Rejoinder." *Tulane Law Review* 46 (1972): 628.

Baudouin, Jean. "Impact of Common Law in Louisiana and Quebec." In *The Role of Judicial Decisions and Doctrine in Civil Law and Mixed Jurisdictions.* Edited by Joseph Dainow. Baton Rouge: Louisiana State University Press, 1974.

Billings, Warren M. "A Course of Studies: Books That Shaped Louisiana Law."

In *A Law unto Itself? Essays in the New Louisiana Legal History,* edited by Warren M. Billings and Mark F. Fernandez. Baton Rouge: Louisiana State University Press, 2001.

———. "From This Seed: The Louisiana Constitution of 1812." In *In Search of Fundamental Law: Louisiana's Constitutions, 1812–1974,* edited by Warren M. Billings and Edward F. Haas. Lafayette: Center for Louisiana Studies, University of Southwestern Louisiana, 1993.

———. "Louisiana Legal History and Its Sources: Needs, Opportunities, and Approaches." In *Louisiana's Legal Heritage,* edited by Edward F. Haas. New Orleans: Perdido Bay Press, 1983.

———. "Origins of Criminal Law in Louisiana." *Louisiana History* 32 (winter 1991): 63–76.

———, and Mark F. Fernandez, eds. *A Law unto Itself? Essays in the New Louisiana Legal History.* Baton Rouge: Louisiana State University Press, 2001.

———, and Edward F. Haas, eds. *In Search of Fundamental Law: Louisiana's Constitutions, 1812–1974.* Lafayette: Center for Louisiana Studies, University of Southwestern Louisiana, 1993.

———, and Judith Kelleher Schafer, eds. *An Uncommon Experience: Law and Judicial Institutions in Louisiana, 1803–2003.* Lafayette: Center for Louisiana Studies, University of Southwestern Louisiana, 1997.

Bonquois, Dora J. "The Career of Henry Adams Bullard: Louisiana Jurist, Legislator, and Educator." *Louisiana Historical Quarterly* 22 (October 1940): 999–1107.

Brasseaux, Carl A. *Denis-Nicolas Foucault and the New Orleans Rebellion of 1768.* McGinty Monograph Series. Ruston, La.: McGinty Publications, 1987.

———. *The Founding of New Acadia: The Beginnings of Acadian Life in Louisiana, 1765–1803.* Baton Rouge: Louisiana State University Press, 1987.

Brown, Elizabeth Gaspar. "Law and Government in the Louisiana Purchase: 1803–1804." *Wayne Law Review* 2 (1956): 169–89.

———. "Legal Systems in Conflict: Orleans Territory, 1804–1812." *American Journal of Legal History* 1 (1957): 35–75.

Bryson, W. Hamilton. *Legal Education in Virginia: 1779–1979: A Biographical Approach.* Charlottesville: University Press of Virginia, 1982.

Carter, Clarence E. "The Office of Commander-in-Chief: A Phase of Imperial Unity on the Eve of the Revolution." In *The Era of the American Revolution: Studies Inscribed to Evarts Boutell Greene,* edited by Richard B. Morris. New York: Columbia University Press, 1939.

Chandler, Richard E., trans. and ed. "The End of an Odyssey: Acadians Arrive at St. Gabriel, Louisiana." *Louisiana History* 14 (winter 1973): 69–87.

Cook, Charles M. *The American Codification Movement: A Study of Antebellum Legal Reform.* Westport, Conn.: Greenwood Press, 1981.

Cortada, James W. "Pierre Rost-Denis and Confederate Diplomacy: A Reevaluation." *Louisiana Historical Review* 54 (1971): 18–27.

Cullen, Charles T. "Completing the Revisal of the Laws in Post-Revolutionary Virginia." *Virginia Magazine of History and Biography* 82 (1974): 84–99.

Cummins, Light T. "Anglo Merchants in Spanish New Orleans: Capital Migration and the Atlantic Economy, 1760–1803." Paper presented to the 53rd Meeting of the Southern Historical Association, New Orleans, 1987.

Dainow, Joseph, ed. *The Role of Judicial Decisions and Doctrine in Civil Law and Mixed Jurisdictions.* Baton Rouge: Louisiana State University Press, 1974.

Dargo, George: *Jefferson's Louisiana: Politics and the Clash of Legal Traditions.* Cambridge, Mass.: Harvard University Press, 1975.

Dart, Benjamin Wall. *Constitutions of the State of Louisiana and Select Federal Laws.* Indianapolis: Bobbs-Merrill, 1932.

Dart, Henry Plauché. "The History of the Louisiana Supreme Court." *Louisiana Historical Quarterly* 4 (1921): 36.

———. "The Legal Institutions of Louisiana." *Louisiana Historical Quarterly* 2 (January 1919): 72–103.

Dart, William K. "The Justices of the Supreme Court." *Louisiana Historical Quarterly* 4 (1921).

Diggins, John Patrick. "The Misuses of Gramsci." *Journal of American History* 75 (June 1988): 141–5.

Din, Gilbert C., and John E. Harkins. *The New Orleans Cabildo: Colonial Louisiana's First City Government, 1769–1803.* Baton Rouge: Louisiana State University Press, 1996.

Evans, Harry Howard. "James Robb, Banker and Pioneer Railroad Builder of Ante Bellum Louisiana." *Louisiana Historical Quarterly* 23 (January 1940): 170–259.

Everard, Wayne M. "Louisiana's 'Whig' Constitution Revisited: The Constitution of 1852." In *In Search of Fundamental Law: Louisiana's Constitutions, 1812–1974,* edited by Warren M. Billings and Edward F. Haas. Lafayette: Center For Louisiana Studies, University of Southwestern Louisiana, 1993.

Fernandez, Mark F. "From Chaos to Continuity: Early Reforms of the Supreme Court of Louisiana, 1845–1852." *Louisiana History* 28 (winter 1987): 19–36.

———. "Local Justice in the Territory of Orleans: W. C. C. Claiborne's Courts,

Judges, and Justices of the Peace." In *A Law unto Itself? Essays in the New Louisiana Legal History,* edited by Warren M. Billings and Mark F. Fernandez. Baton Rouge: Louisiana State University Press, 2001.

————. "Rules of Court of the Territory of Orleans." *Louisiana History* 38 (winter 1997): 63–73.

————. *"State v. McLean et al.:* Louisiana's First History of Criminal Law." *Louisiana History* 37 (summer 1995): 313–25.

————. "The Appellate Question: A Comparative Analysis of Supreme Courts of Appeal in Virginia and Louisiana, 1776–1840." Ph.D. diss., College of William and Mary in Virginia, 1991.

Friedman, Lawrence M. *American Law: An Introduction.* New York: W. W. Norton, 1984.

Gaspard, Elizabeth. "Rise of the Louisiana Bar." *Louisiana History* 28 (spring 1987): 183–93.

Genovese, Eugene D. *Roll Jordan Roll.* New York: Pantheon Books, 1975.

Greene, Jack P., and J. R. Pole, eds. *Colonial British America: Essays in the New History of the Early Modern Era.* Baltimore: Johns Hopkins University Press, 1984.

Greene, Jack P. *Peripheries and Center: Constitutional Development in the Extended Polities of the British Empire and the United States, 1607–1788.* Athens: University of Georgia Press, 1986.

Groner, Samuel B. "Louisiana Law: Its Development in the First Quarter Century of American Rule." *Louisiana Law Review* 8 (January 1948), 350–462.

Hardy, James D., Jr. "The Superior Council in Colonial Louisiana." In *Frenchmen and French Ways in the Mississippi Valley,* edited by Francis McDermott. Urbana: University of Illinois Press, 1969.

Hatcher, William B. *Edward Livingston: Jeffersonian Republican and Jacksonian Democrat.* Baton Rouge: Louisiana State University Press, 1940.

Hatfield, Joseph T. *William Claiborne: Jeffersonian Centurion in the American Southwest.* Lafayette: Center for Louisiana Studies, University of Southwestern Louisiana, 1976.

Hood, John T. "The Louisiana Judiciary." *Louisiana Law Review* 14 (1954): 811–24.

Hurst, James Willard. *The Growth of American Law: The Lawmakers.* Boston: Little Brown, 1950.

Johnson, Alan, et al., eds. *The Dictionary of American Biography.* New York: Charles Scribner's Sons, 1958.

Johnson, Jerah. *"Les Coutumes de Paris,* Louisiana's First Law." *Louisiana History* 30 (spring 1984): 145–55.

Jordan, Winthrop D. *White over Black: American Attitudes toward the Negro, 1550– 1812.* Chapel Hill: University of North Carolina Press, 1968. Reprint, New York: W. W. Norton, 1997.

Haas, Edward F. *Louisiana's Legal Heritage.* New Orleans: Perdido Bay Press, 1983.

Kammen, Michael. *Colonial New York: A History.* White Plains, N.Y.: KTO Press, 1975.

Kilbourne, Richard H., Jr. *A History of the Louisiana Civil Code: The Formative Years, 1803–1839.* Baton Rouge: Louisiana State University Press, 1987.

———. "An Overview of the Work of the Territorial Court, 1804–1809: A Missing Chapter in the Development of the Louisiana Civil Code." In *Louisiana's Legal Heritage,* edited by Edward F. Haas. New Orleans: Perdido Bay Press, 1983.

Lears, T. J. Jackson, "The Concept of Cultural Hegemony: Problems and Possibilities." *American Historical Review* 90 (June 1988): 567–94.

Leff, Arthur A. "Injury, Ignorance, and Spite—The Dynamics of Coercive Collection." *Yale Law Journal* 80 (November 1970): 1–46.

Lemieux, Donald Jile. "The Office of *Commissaire Ordonnateur* in French Louisiana, 1731–1763: A Study in French Colonial Administration." Ph.D. diss., Baton Rouge, Louisiana State University, 1972.

Lester, Dick M. "John Dick of New Orleans." *Louisiana History* 34 (summer 1993): 357–66.

Lyons, E. Wilson. *Louisiana in French Diplomacy, 1759–1804.* Norman: University of Oklahoma Press, 1934.

Lyons, Grant. "Livingston and the Louisiana Criminal Codes." *Louisiana History* 15 (summer 1974): 243–72.

———. "Narrow Failure, Wider Triumph." Master's thesis, University of New Orleans, 1973.

McDermott, John Francis, ed. *Frenchmen and French Ways in the Mississippi Valley.* Urbana: University of Illinois Press, 1969.

Micelle, Jerry A. "From Law Court to Local Government: Metamorphosis of the Superior Council of French Louisiana." *Louisiana History* 9 (spring 1968): 85–107.

Miller, Ben Robertson. *The Louisiana Judiciary.* University Studies no. 9. Baton Rouge: Louisiana State University Press, 1932.

Miller, F. Thornton. *Juries and Judges Versus the Law: Virginia's Provincial Legal Perspective, 1783–1828*. Charlottesville: University Press of Virginia, 1994.

Moore, John Preston. "Antonio de Ulloa: A Profile of the First Spanish Governor of Louisiana." *Louisiana History* 8 (summer 1967): 189–219.

————. *Revolt in Louisiana: The Spanish Occupation, 1766–1770*. Baton Rouge: Louisiana State University Press, 1976.

Morgan, Gwenda. *The Hegemony of the Law: Richmond County, Virginia, 1692–1776*. New York: Garland Publishing, 1989.

Newton, Lewis William. *The Americanization of French Louisiana: A Study in American Populations in Louisiana, 1803–1860*. New York: Arno Press, 1980.

O'Neal, F. Hodge. "An Appraisal of the Louisiana Law of Partnership." *Louisiana Law Review* 9 (1948–1949): 307–409, 450–45.

O'Neill, Charles Edwards. *Church and State in French Colonial Louisiana: Policy and Politics to 1732*. New Haven, Conn.: Yale University Press, 1966.

Paschal, Robert A. "Sources of the Digest of 1808: A Reply to Professor Batiza." *Tulane Law Review* 46 (1972): 603–52.

Remini, Robert V. *Andrew Jackson*. New York: Harper and Row, 1966.

Roeber, A. G. *Faithful Magistrates and Republican Lawyers: Creators of Virginia's Legal Culture, 1680–1810*. Chapel Hill: University of North Carolina Press in Association with the Institute of Early American History and Culture, 1981.

Schafer, Judith K. "Reform or Experiment? The Constitution of 1845." In *In Search of Fundamental Law: Louisiana's Constitutions, 1812–1974*, edited by Warren M. Billings and Edward F. Haas. Lafayette: Center for Louisiana Studies, University of Southwestern Louisiana, 1993.

Speck, W. A. "The International and Imperial Context." In *Colonial British America Essays in the New History of the Early Modern Era*, edited by Jack P. Greene and J. R. Pole. Baltimore: Johns Hopkins University Press, 1984.

Tate, Albert, Jr. "The Role of the Judge in Mixed Jurisdictions." In *The Role of Judicial Decisions and Doctrine in Civil Law and Mixed Jurisdictions*, edited by Joseph Dainow. Baton Rouge: Louisiana State University Press, 1974.

Taylor, Joe Gray. *Louisiana: A Bicentennial History*. New York: W. W. Norton, 1976.

Texada, David Ker. *Alejandro O'Reilly and the New Orleans Rebels*. Lafayette: Center for Louisiana Studies, University of Southwestern Louisiana, 1970.

Thompson, E. P. *Whigs and Hunters: The Origin of the Black Act*. New York: Pantheon, 1975.

Tregle, Joseph G., Jr. *Louisiana in the Age of Jackson: A Clash of Cultures and Personalities*. Baton Rouge: Louisiana State University Press, 1999.

Usner, Daniel. *Indians, Settlers, and Slaves in a Frontier Exchange Economy: The Lower Mississippi Valley before 1783.* Chapel Hill: University of North Carolina Press, 1992.

VanBurkleo, Sandra F. "'That Our Pure Republican Principles Might Not Whither': Kentucky's Relief Crisis and the Pursuit of 'Moral Justice,'" 1818–1826. Ph.D. diss., University of Minnesota, 1988.

Watson, Alan. *The Evolution of Law.* Baltimore: Johns Hopkins University Press, 1985.

Williams, William H. "The History of Carrollton." *Louisiana Historical Quarterly* 22 (January 1939): 181–216.

Young, Sheridan E. "Louisiana's Court of Errors and Appeals, 1843–1846." In *A Law unto Itself? Essays in the New Louisiana Legal History,* edited by Warren M. Billings and Mark F. Fernandez. Baton Rouge: Louisiana State University Press, 2001.

INDEX